Self-Publishing

A Step-by-step Beginner's Guide Creating and Self-publishing

(The Secret Guide to Becoming a Best Seller)

Nathan Webb

Published By **Simon Dough**

Nathan Webb

All Rights Reserved

Self-Publishing: A Step-by-step Beginner's Guide Creating and Self-publishing (The Secret Guide to Becoming a Best Seller)

ISBN 978-1-7773679-3-0

No part of this guidebook shall be reproduced in any form without permission in writing from the publisher except in the case of brief quotations embodied in critical articles or reviews.

Legal & Disclaimer

The information contained in this book is not designed to replace or take the place of any form of medicine or professional medical advice. The information in this book has been provided for educational & entertainment purposes only.

The information contained in this book has been compiled from sources deemed reliable, and it is accurate to the best of the Author's knowledge; however, the Author cannot guarantee its accuracy and validity and cannot be held liable for any errors or omissions. Changes are periodically made to this book. You must consult your doctor or get professional medical advice before using any of the suggested remedies, techniques, or information in this book.

Upon using the information contained in this book, you agree to hold harmless the Author from and against any damages, costs, and expenses, including any legal fees potentially resulting from the application of any of the information provided by this guide. This disclaimer applies to any damages or injury caused by the use and application, whether directly or indirectly, of any advice or information presented, whether for breach of contract, tort, negligence, personal injury, criminal intent, or under any other cause of action.

You agree to accept all risks of using the information presented inside this book. You need to consult a professional medical practitioner in order to ensure you are both able and healthy enough to participate in this program.

Table Of Contents

Chapter 1: Why Self-Publish? 1

Chapter 2: The File Storage For Kdp 20

Chapter 3: The Best Practices 33

Chapter 4: Titles And Subbtitles 43

Chapter 5: Reaching Your Target Audience 54

Chapter 6: Achieving A Positive Reader Experience 67

Chapter 7: Social Media Marketing 82

Chapter 8: The Most Money Selling Kindle Ebooks 119

Chapter 9: Write An Ebook To Be Used On Amazon Kindle 135

Chapter 10: Writing An Ebook 147

Chapter 11: Pros And Cons Of Selling Amazon Kindle Ebooks 156

Chapter 12: The Advertising Your Amazon Kindle Ebook 173

Chapter 1: Why Self-Publish?

Self-publishing through KDP offers a number of advantages over traditional publishing. There are seven good reasons:

Control of creativity: When self-publishing authors have the full creative control of their own work. They are able to make modifications to the cover of their book and blurb whenever they feel appropriate, and not have to wait for input from the publisher.

Speedier turnaround: Traditional publishing could take several months, or even years to put an item on the market. Self-publishing with KDP the authors will have their books available for purchase within a few days.

Higher royalty rates The traditional publishers generally give authors a royalty that is between 10-15% of amount of their cover, and self-published authors could receive as much as 70% of the price they sell on KDP.

Distribution across the globe: KDP provides authors with the possibility to connect with readers from countries across the globe without the requirement for an editor to sign international rights agreements.

Access to sales information Authors with self-published books through KDP are able to access live sales statistics, which could aid them in making informed choices regarding promotional and marketing strategies.

There are no gatekeepers: In the traditional method of publishing, author usually need to undergo lengthy and tedious application process. Even at the end, they might get rejected by publishers that aren't convinced there is a demand for their writing. Self-publishing with KDP will eliminate these barriers and lets authors connect with the readers directly.

Higher profit margins: Since self-published authors using KDP maintain greater influence over the work they create, and are able to earn more royalties They have the chance to make more as opposed to authors who choose through the traditional publishing process.

However, self-publishing doesn't come completely free of obstacles. The authors who go the self-publishing route must assume a lot of tasks that traditional publishers handle like designing and editing covers, and even marketing. With the appropriate devices and information self-publishing with KDP could be a rewarding and lucrative project for authors.

OFTEN ASKED QUESTIONS

Self-publishing through Amazon KDP has grown increasing popular in recent times and with reasons that are well-founded. Thanks to its easy-to-use platform and worldwide coverage, Amazon KDP offers writers the chance to publish your work in a matter of minutes and speed. As with every venture there's a lot of concerns that writers might be faced with prior to embarking on the self-publishing path. Here are a list of most commonly asked questions regarding self-publishing with Amazon KDP:

What exactly is Amazon KDP? Amazon KDP stands for Kindle Direct Publishing and is a self-publishing system which allows authors to publish their work in both the print and electronic formats. Amazon KDP provides a streamlined procedure for authors to release and publish their work through Amazon the biggest online marketplace.

What's the price to create a book for Amazon KDP? Amazon KDP does not charge the author upfront costs to make a book available on its platform. Authors only pay when their book is sold which results in Amazon getting a share of the profits. Printing and shipping physical copies of the book may be a part of the royalty.

What kinds of books can be published on Amazon KDP? Amazon KDP allows authors to publish an array of book types, including poetry, fiction, nonfiction as well as children's and young adult books as well as many others. But, Amazon KDP does have specific content guidelines to be adhered to, for example restricting the publication of books with explicit or illegal or offensive content.

Do I require an ISBN for publishing my work on Amazon KDP? An ISBN (International Standard Book Number) isn't required for publishing in Amazon KDP. Amazon KDP provides a free ISBN for books printed in print, and digital books don't need an ISBN.

What's the average time to get a book published through Amazon KDP? The length of time required for the book to be released via Amazon KDP depends on a range of elements like the size of the book structure, as well as the quality of the document. In general, it takes anything from a few hours up to a few days for books to become available for purchase on Amazon once it is uploaded to the KDP platform.

What kind of royalties could I anticipate by self-publishing through Amazon KDP? Amazon KDP offers a competitive royalty structure with authors getting as much as 70% of the price list for digital books, and as high as 60% for printed books. The actual royalty rate is contingent upon a variety of variables like pricing, location of the sale and the extent to which the book is included into specific programs like Kindle Unlimited.

What can I do to promote my book Amazon KDP? Amazon KDP offers a range of tools and resources for authors to promote their book, including making author profiles, launching marketing campaigns and making use of Amazon's marketing platform. In addition, authors are able to utilize social media along with other channels of online marketing to boost their book's exposure and sales.

Self-publishing through Amazon KDP offers writers a unique chance to showcase their writing with an international public. Thanks to its easy-to-use platform with competitive royalties as well as vast promotional tools Amazon KDP is now the preferred choice for authors who want to self-publish their work. There are initially-posed questions however, self-publishing with Amazon KDP could be extremely rewarding for authors of every level.

BETA READERS

The process of writing a book can be an intense, solitary task It's not difficult to lose yourself within your own writing. This is where beta readers step into the picture. Beta readers are people who reviews the first draft of the book and gives feedback prior to it being released. This chapter will look at the significance of beta readers in the publication of a novel.

A Fresh View: As the author of your novel You are close to the book to have an objective view. An editor or a beta reader could provide fresh eyes as well as provide an impartial view on the work you've put into it. They are able to identify problems could have gone unnoticed for instance issues with pacing, plot holes or any inconsistencies within the story.

Comments regarding Style and tone: Beta readers are able to provide feedback to your style and tone of writing. They can let you know whether your writing is entertaining and believable, whether your dialogue is authentic, or if your characters have a sense of. The feedback you receive can help enhance your writing and make an engaging reader experience for your readers.

Identify issues with the plot The help of beta readers is to you spot plot flaws which may not immediately evident. They'll be able to point out when your tale is predictable or has characters that aren't making sense. The feedback they provide can help to improve the story's structure to make it more appealing.

Check your audience's demographic Test your target audience with beta readers. They can provide an insight into your readership. If your book is written targeted at a particular category of people like romantic readers or young adults Beta readers of this group can inform whether your novel is a hit with people in that group. The feedback they provide can help you adapt your story to the audience you're targeting and sure you're meeting the requirements.

Find spelling and grammar mistakes The beta reader can assist you in catching grammar and spelling mistakes. Though this isn't the sole reason you should use beta readers, it's an essential benefit. The more polished your work is and the more professional your manuscript will look to publishers and other readers.

Create relationships with beta readers: They could become your greatest advocates. If they are satisfied with your novel and are satisfied, they will likely suggest it to relatives and friends. Additionally, they can leave glowing reviews on platforms online that can boost the visibility of your book and assist to build your fan base.

Beta readers provide valuable information about the story's structure as well as the pacing of the story characters' development and the dialogue. They also can help to identify gaps in the plot, inconsistencies or areas that require greater detail or clarification. Beta readers provide authors with an understanding of the way their intended audience will be impacted by the novel. These feedbacks can be utilized to alter the book's content before releasing the book to the general public.

Beta readers are also able to provide encouragement and emotional support to authors throughout the process of writing. The process of writing a book is very lonely, and authors are prone to lose their sense of self-respect when they've spent so long writing their work. Readers from the beta group can give new perspectives and aid writers remain on the right track by providing them with the motivation that they require to complete their project.

They're an integral part in the process of writing a book. They are able to provide helpful critique, help identify problems which need to be resolved as well as provide emotional support for authors. In the end writers should think about using beta readers in order to make the perfect book. If it's a novel that is debut or a well-known author's most recent project, beta readers could assist in making a book as good as it can be.

The bottom line is that beta readers are an essential component of writing. They offer valuable comments and provide a fresh viewpoint on your work. Beta readers will help you find plot flaws, improve your writing style as well as spot spelling and grammar mistakes. They will also offer insights into the audience you want to reach and assist you in building connections with readers who might be interested. Therefore, if you're an aspiring author you should think about having beta readers aid you in writing the best potential version of your book.

COVERS FOR BOOKS

One of the key factors of self-publishing your book is having a professional cover layout. The book's cover is the first thing that a prospective reader is exposed to and it can influence their decision to buy the book. There are five main reasons the use of a professional design and layout is essential:

First impressions are important the cover of a book can be the first thing that a prospective viewer sees and will influence whether they decide whether to purchase the book or not. The design of a professional book's cover will draw the attention of a potential reader and encourage them to buy the book to learn more about the subject.

Communicating the correct message The design for the cover must convey the tone and style of the novel, in addition to the readers. An experienced book cover designer will ensure that the cover precisely conveys the purpose of the book, and also attracts the readership you want to reach.

Make your mark in a competitive market. There are millions of books to choose from on Amazon as well as having an attractive book cover helps a book stand out from the crowd. An original and attractive cover design will help your book stand out to people who might be interested in it and boost your chances of making a sale.

Marketing and branding Covers for books that are professionally designed design could also aid in branding and marketing strategies. The design of a well-designed cover is employed across various channels for marketing including the internet, emails announcements, newsletters, and advertising. A consistent branding style can aid in building credibility and confidence among prospective users.

Improve perceived value The professional appearance of a book's cover design could increase the value perception of the book. Covers that are well-designed can convey the impression that the product is of high quality and is worth the money. It can result in higher numbers of sales, and also positive reviews from the readers.

Professionally designed covers for books is a crucial aspect to consider when self-publishing books. This can assist to make a book stand out from an incredibly competitive market, communicate the correct message to potential viewers, help with the branding and marketing effort as well as increase its value to the public. book. The hiring of a professional book cover designer can be a wise purchase for anyone self-published who wants to make a great book.

Select"Sign in" and then click the "Sign Up" button. The button is at the upper right part of the display, it is also possible to select "Sign in" If your already registered for the Amazon account.

Input your email address as well as your password. Also, you must select the language you prefer and then agree to the conditions and terms.

Click"Create your KDP account" or click on the "Create Your KDP Account" button.

Then, you will have to furnish additional details like your name, address and telephone number. These details are required to ensure you receive taxes and royalty forms.

After you've provided the data, you'll be directed to your KDP dashboard. It is here that you will be able to organize your accounts and keep track of the sales you make.

It's now time to start uploading your books on Amazon KDP. Prior to doing this, however it's best to be familiar with the guidelines and policies of KDP. The information can be found through the "Help" button located in the upper right part of the display, or visiting the KDP FAQ page on the website.

Following these steps, you'll be able make the Amazon KDP account and start the procedure of uploading your book onto the site.

Best Practices To create your KDP Account

Utilize an Professional Email Address: When making the Amazon KDP account, use an email address that is professional. Avoid using personal or casual email addresses like "funnybunny1234@gmail.com" or "cutiepie@hotmail.com". Instead, create an email address that uses your name or your pen name, such as "jane.doe.author@gmail.com".

Make sure you choose a password that is strong Select a password that is tough to remember. Choose a mix of lower and uppercase characters, numbers as well as symbols. Don't use easily identifiable details like your name, birth date, or even your phone number.

Maintain Your Account Information Current Check that the information on your account is current which includes your names, addresses, and information about your payment. It ensures you get payments on time and the readers of your account can get in touch with your account if they need to.

Be sure to read and adhere to Amazon KDP's Guidelines before uploading your book, be sure that you have read and understood the guidelines of Amazon KDP. It will guarantee your book's approval and meets specifications for formatting.

Chapter 2: The File Storage For Kdp

When you are ready to upload your book to Amazon, you'll be required to make your book's file. Amazon KDP accepts the following formats for files: Microsoft Word (.docx), HTML, EPUB, and Kindle Create (.kpf). The format of your book must be adapted to your book in accordance with Amazon's guidelines. These guidelines are available on the KDP site.

Prepare your book in order to submit it for Amazon KDP

Prior to uploading your manuscript to Amazon KDP to be read by the KDP, you have to check that it has been properly formatted. It will make sure your book appears professional and easy to browse on the Kindle device or through the Kindle application. These are the steps you need to take:

Select the file format you prefer: Amazon KDP accepts several formats for files, such as Microsoft Word, ePub, and KPF.

Create your document Before beginning to format the book, you'll be required to layout your documents in the right method. It involves setting the margins, choosing the right font and size while ensuring the document is correctly aligned.

Page breaks are important to make sure that your book is structured correctly it is necessary to create page breaks in between sections and chapters. This ensures that your book is straightforward to read and navigate.

The addition of headings to your books can make it easier for your readers to follow and locate the information they're seeking. Make use of headings to separate sections or chapters, and makes your book less difficult to browse through.

Images In the event that your book includes photographs, you'll have to make sure that they're well-formatted and optimized to view on the Kindle device or Kindle app. Images must be in JPEG or PNG format, and must not be larger than 10MB.

Verify your formatting: Prior to you publish your book on Amazon KDP It is essential that you check the formatting of your book for errors to ensure everything appears perfect. Check for any typos in the text, formatting issues, and other problems that may impact the reading experience of your work.

When you've finished the formatting of your book, make certain to save your book using the correct formats for your file. I suggest keeping a backup copy of your work on a different location like an USB drive or cloud storage for the event that you have to edit your book later.

If you follow these instructions by following these guidelines, you'll be able prepare your book to be suitable for Amazon KDP and ensure that your book looks professional and simple to read using either a Kindle device, or via the Kindle application.

Best Practices

How to prepare your book's files for uploading onto Amazon KDP

Select the right file format: Amazon KDP accepts a range of formats for files that include DOC, DOCX HTML, HTML, MOBI EPUB RTF PDF, KPF. But, you should pick the one which is the most suitable for the book you're writing. If, for instance, the book has images or graphics, you should choose either PDF or KPF so they're displayed correctly.

Utilize a Standard Font Choose a font that is standard such as Times New Roman or Arial for the text of your book. This will guarantee that your book will be easy to read and is compatible with various gadgets.

Create a professional book format Formatting your book correctly is crucial for reading comprehension and the overall design of the book. Make use of headings, subheadings as well as bullets, to separate the text, making it more easy to comprehend. Use pages that break between chapters or sections to make sure that your work is organized.

Create a table of contents A table of contents will make it much easier for your readers to follow the flow of your text. Utilize headings and subheadings in order to make a hierarchical structure that's easy to adhere to.

Make sure to check for Spelling and Grammar Mistakes: Spelling and grammar errors are distracting and could cause your book to look less professional. Make use of a spell-checker, and make sure your book is proofread before uploading into Amazon KDP.

Examine Your Book Test Your Book on Multiple Devices Check your work on various devices and platforms to make sure that the book reads and looks smoothly on every one of them. Utilize the Amazon Kindle Previewer or other tools to check your book's performance on various devices and adjust it as needed.

Include the Copyright Page: Include a copyright page near the start of your book, which contains crucial information such as the book's title, author's name, copyright year, as well as the publisher's information.

Following these top practices You can be sure that your book has been properly formatted and ready to be uploaded into Amazon KDP. This will make sure that your book looks professional and will be well-received by people who read it.

Pick the book type you'd like to write by selecting from the available options (there could be more available in the near future). It is possible to choose between Paperback, Kindle eBook or hardcover. You can include these in your existing book at any time.

The general setup will be the same for each of the three formats, and so I'll presume that you're creating an ebook cover however, I'll go into the distinctions between print and ebook print in the future.

Language: This is where the language used in the book will be If you are using different languages you want to use for your novel later it is possible to add them in the following set-up.

The subtitle and title of your book are among the first items readers look at. It is important to ensure that the title of your book is simple, clear, and conveys the message of the book. Also, you should think about adding a subtitle which provides additional information about the topic of your book.

If you're planning your book to form an element of a larger series or you believe it might become part of a series even though it's not yet intended, then you may add this option to the list. It is also possible to add this to your manuscript when you are ready.

The edition feature lets you upgrade the previously published book you have on Amazon KDP. There is no need to submit this form in the case of this being the first edition you've made of the book you've written.

Include the name of the author in the book. Alternatively, you could use the pen name.

In the description section It's essential to provide an engaging overview of your book. Though this overview doesn't have to match that found in the book's back cover the book, you'll be able to reduce time and effort with the same format. Make sure you use the formatting tools like bold, italic and underline, to help your words stand out as well as consider adding bullet points that split large sections of text. In addition, adding beta reader reviews will provide social proof as well as convince prospective customers to take a look at your novel the chance. Therefore, take your time to create a professionally written and structured description that includes appealing reviews. This will give your novel the greatest chances to be successful with Amazon KDP.

If you plan to publish your book via Amazon KDP It is crucial to select the right publishing rights options. This can help safeguard the intellectual property of your book and avoid future legal issues later on. It is also important to confirm that all the information in your publication is what you're entitled to make use of. If you're dealing with materials that are in the public domain and you aren't concerned about readers having access to it for free it's possible to select the same option. When you choose the right publication rights choice and insuring the content of your book is legal and sound it will prepare your book to be successful and steer clear of possible legal issues.

Select your 7 keywords below and reference the next chapters to learn about the best practices on which words to pick.

The selection of the appropriate areas is vital to making certain that your book will be read by the correct target audience. Amazon lets you choose two categories to showcase your book. Be sure to select categories that reflect accurately your book's content.

If your book is intended toward children, it is possible to specify the child's age and grade interval within this section. This helps parents and teachers to find the books for their kids.

If you'd like to open your book for pre-orders, you may decide on a release date and offer it for pre-orders as long as 90 days prior to the release date.

The uploading process is when you submit your work for ebook. The most common formats to upload is an EPUB file however, you may prepare the book with Kindle Create and upload a KPF file. It is also recommended to turn off DRM to protect your book from being lost or distributed via the internet.

Put your book's cover into this box. It is highly recommended not making use of the Cover Creator create a cover on your own in the event that your book is one you do not plan on marketing and selling to others. There are many internet tools to design your own book covers. Also, you can contact our partner via ilovemycover.com to receive assistance.

Review your book here and find any flaws. If any of the parts in this book not correct or contain errors, they will be displayed here within the previewer.

A ISBN (International Standard Book Number) is an unique identifier to identify your book. If you own an ISBN, then you are able to add it to this page. If you don't own any ISBN, Amazon will provide an ISBN for you.

Kindle eBook Pricing

If you're using KDP Select, I would advise that all authors join in this program, since it's the best way to receive publicity and opinions about your work from those who might otherwise be hesitant to buy it directly.

Chapter 3: The Best Practices

To set up your Book for setting up your Book Amazon KDP

Pick a meaningful and engaging name: Your title must accurately reflect the contents and be appealing to your intended audience. It must be engaging and easy to recall and distinctive.

Design a striking cover The cover of your book should look appealing, and professional created to entice viewers. It must be high-resolution, as well as in JPEG or TIFF format.

Make a compelling book's description: The description should give a concise description of your book's content and encourage readers to buy the book. Be sure to use the keywords and phrases pertinent to the book's genre as well as the subject.

Choose the right categories and keywords Pick categories and keyword that are precise in describing your work and assist potential readers locate the book. There is the option of selecting up to 10 categories as well as 7 keywords So, make sure you choose carefully.

Review your book prior to publishing Make use of Amazon's previewer to make sure that your work is well-designed and doesn't contain any errors. The tool lets you examine how your work appears on various gadgets, and can assist you in identifying formatting mistakes or mistakes.

Utilize Amazon's formatting guidelines: Amazon has specific formatting guidelines you must be following to ensure that your work looks professional, and also easily understand. The guidelines include how to format your text, images as well as tables.

Make your book search-friendly by optimizing it for engines. Use appropriate keywords within your book's titles, descriptions, and metadata so that it will appear in the search results. It can assist potential buyers locate your book faster.

Make your profile an author's page Make an author profile on Amazon to market your book, and to connect to readers. You should include a bio, picture as well as hyperlinks to your site and your social media accounts.

Following these top practices by following these best practices, you will improve the visibility of your book and attract potential readers through Amazon KDP.

Content in Paperback and Hardcover

If you are planning to publish the print edition of your work through Amazon KDP and KDP, it's vital to have the ISBN (International Standard Book Number). An

ISBN is an unique identification number that enables libraries, booksellers as well as distributors to find the book they want to purchase. KDP has a cost-free ISBN service for authors however it's crucial to know that this ISBN can only be valid via Amazon. If you are planning to market the book beyond Amazon you should buy your ISBN from the ISBN authority within your nation. When you purchase an ISBN increases the exposure and popularity of your publication, making it simpler for customers to purchase and find the book. Furthermore, having an ISBN is necessary in certain promotions, like being included on the Books in Print database or getting considered for book reviews published by major publications.

In printing your paperback book via Amazon KDP it is essential to think about the kind of paper and ink used. The two primary choices of ink for printing with

KDP are white and black or full-color. Printing in black and white generally is more economical which makes it an ideal choice for texts-heavy books. If your work contains photos or illustrations it could be required to present the work in a professional manner. Also, the kind of paper is a factor in the appearance and the feel of the book. KDP provides two primary papers that are white and cream. White paper tends to be more sharp and brighter, whereas cream paper is older, traditional look. In the end, your choice of papers and inks will be based on the look and layout of the book along with your budget and the intended audience. You should consider each option, and then choose the best combination to showcase your writing while staying within the limits of your budget.

If you are uploading a print-ready version of your PDF file to Amazon KDP, one important aspect to consider is the trim dimension of your book. The size of the trim refers to the dimensions that will be finalized for your book when it's been printed and then trimmed. Amazon KDP offers a range of sizes that you can choose from, which include traditional sizes such as 6" 9" and 8.5" 11.5" in addition to different sizes for different types of books.

The size of the trim you select could affect the overall look and the feel of your book in addition to the price. The smaller sizes of trim that are smaller, like 5" 8" could be smaller and more economical and therefore a preferred selection for novels and other books of fiction. More substantial trim sizes, for example 8.5" 11" are usually employed for manuals, textbooks and non-fiction publications which may need more room to include illustrations or diagrams.

It's crucial to pick the appropriate size of trim of your book, based on the genre, contents, and the intended readership. The right trim size will help your book appear more visually appealing as well as easier to read, as well as giving it a professional appearance and experience. While designing your book's internal layout, you should be aware of the trim size you've chosen in mind. This is because the design and formatting will have to be adjusted in line with the trim size.

Alongside trimming the dimensions, you need to take into consideration other factors in your printed book like the cover design and paper style. If you take care to consider these elements to create an excellent printed book that is appealing to the readers, and allow you to make a mark in an increasingly competitive market.

When you upload your PDF file to print using KDP It is crucial to take into consideration the settings for bleed. Bleed means the portion that is not part of the dimensions of your publication where the design must be extended to prevent any unnecessary blank space, or the cutting of vital components. The standard bleed size for KDP can be set to 0.125 inches, or 3.2 millimeters. However, it's important to verify the specifications for your particular trimming size since they could differ. It is important to configure your bleed using your design software prior to exporting the PDF file for uploading to KDP. When you spend the time to setup your bleed you will ensure that the printed book appears elegant and professional.

There is also the possibility to pick the finishing of your book. The design and feel of the book's cover. This will affect the appearance and feel of the book. The options available for covers appearance on KDP includes matte and glossy. Covers with glossy finishes have glossy, reflective surfaces which makes the colors look more vivid While matte covers come with smooth, non-reflective surfaces which gives an elegant and subtle appearance. Selecting the best finish for your book is crucial to make sure that your book is designed with the perfect style and appearance.

The uploading of your manuscript in PDF to KDP is a crucial aspect of self-publishing. After you've formatted and edited the manuscript, you'll have to save it as a PDF document prior to sending it over to KDP. You must ensure that the PDF file is properly formatted, using the correct size of page as well as margins and fonts. KDP offers a useful tutorial to assist you in formatting your book to make sure your book meets their standards. After you have completed your PDF then you can send the file to KDP which allows you to look over your manuscript and make any adjustments prior to publication. Uploading your book to KDP is simple It permits you to make your book available in front of a worldwide public.

In uploading a book cover to print KDP It is crucial to ensure that your image is in compliance with the specifications set by KDP. The requirements include the type of file size, resolution, and type. KDP demands a cover photo to be uploaded in the form of PDF. The image should have at minimum 300 DPI in order to get the highest quality. Also, the image must be of a size that is similar to the dimensions of the book. It should also incorporate a spine when needed.

Chapter 4: Titles And Subbtitles

The title and the subtitle of your publication are two of the most crucial components of your book's overall appearance. They offer readers an overview of the subject matter of your book and could be the decisive element in deciding whether someone chooses to purchase your book or not. In this article I'll go over the significance of having a well-written title and title for your book.

Attracting the attention of the reader

The subtitle and title of your novel are the first items readers notice. The right title and subtitle are sure to draw the attention of readers and draw them in to know more about the book. They must be captivating and unforgettable, and provide the reader with a clear idea of what readers can anticipate from your book.

Establishing expectations

The title and subtitle of your book must accurately represent the contents of the book. It will set the expectations for readers and assure them that they will satisfied with the book's content. If your subtitle and title is misleading, users may get deceived and post negative review.

Creating buzz

An appealing title and subtitle could generate buzz about your book, and create curiosity from readers. If your subtitle and title is intriguing and stimulating readers may want to share your book via social media, or suggest the book to friends and family. This will boost the popularity of your publication and draw many more readers.

Aiding in the search for a better way to be found.

The title and subtitle are crucial in assisting readers to locate the book.

They're crucial components in SEO or search engine optimization (SEO) and will help your book to appear more prominently on search results. If you incorporate relevant keywords into the title and subtitle of your book to increase the visibility of your book and draw more attention to your book.

Establishing your brand

Your subtitle and title could also aid in establishing your name as an author. If the book you write can be part of a larger series using a consistent name pattern for your titles and subtitles may help readers understand the work you write and develop avid followers. This can help to make your name known as a writer. It can also give readers a sense of what they can be expecting from the next work you write.

To conclude, making sure you have a great subtitle and title to your book are essential to draw readers in, creating curiosity, and building your name. Your subtitle and title must be appealing, precise and pertinent to the contents of the book. Also, they should include pertinent keywords to increase discoverability and assist readers in finding your book. By using a well-written book's title as well as a subtitle you'll be able to boost the exposure of your book, and also attract many more readers. This will ultimately lead to better success as a writer.

THE BEST PRACTICES

The Writing of a Title and Subtitle

Clear and succinct: Your title should be clear and concise. It should convey the message of your book Your subtitle must give additional information or context. Be careful not to use confusing or obscure language, which can confuse readers.

Include pertinent keywords in your subtitle and title will help to make your book pop prominently in the search results, as well as make it easier for users to locate. Consider what words or phrases someone could use in searching for books similar to yours.

Make your book compelling and enticing your title and subtitles should spark the interest of readers and make them want find out more. You might consider using intriguing phrases, asking a challenging query, or emphasizing an interesting aspect of the book.

Look up other titles within the genre you are interested in: Read previous books with a high success rate within your field to gain a feel for what is successful and what's not. Look for common patterns, themes or phrases and try to come up with a method to make your book's title and subtitle stand out the rest of the book.

IMPORTANCE of KEYWORDS

Keywords are vital to make your book accessible to possible users via Amazon KDP. Authors need to input keywords relevant to their book when uploading books to KDP so your book will be displayed within relevant search results. The use of keywords can increase the visibility of your book, as well as click-through rates as well as sales. In the end it's important to select keywords that convey the job.

The use of keywords that work well can boost visibility of the book. The algorithm of Amazon determines whether or not a given book can be linked to a particular search question by utilizing the keywords. If the book is relevant to keywords, it'll rank higher on search results which will increase its exposure. This increases the chance of readers coming across this book.

The right choice of keywords can improve the book's Click-through rates. If the book is listed on the results page and the user clicks on the thumbnail image to find more details. Utilizing precise terms that precisely convey the story will draw people looking for books similar to it. The result will be more clicks and indicates that more people are intrigued by the book.

A good keyword can lead to a rise in sales. When a book shows up in the results of a search this increases the chance of people finding the book. People are more likely to purchase a book if its description and the design appeal to them. Utilizing the appropriate keyword phrases in the book's metadata will ensure that the book is read by the correct audience, thus improving the chances of the publication to eventually be bought.

It is essential to conduct research and utilize long-tail keywords. Keywords with a long tail are not as competitive, and also more specific. Since they're more specific They are also less competitive However, they're more precise, which implies that they draw readers who are more likely to purchase the book. The use of long-tail keywords to convey the content of the book may lead to increased sales and an increased conversion rate.

Authors are also required to include key keywords in the title as well as title of their book. This will ensure that the book will be listed in search results that are relevant as well as increases the chances of readers coming across the book. The subtitle and title of the book need to properly represent the text and contain keywords that are relevant to the topic and genre.

When uploading books to Amazon KDP the right keywords are crucial. Making use of appropriate keywords can increase effectiveness, visibility, click-through and also the sales. Therefore the authors must spend some the time to research and select words that are appropriate to the book's content. Incorporating relevant keywords into the title and subtitle along with making use of long-tail keywords aid in promoting the book's popularity and draw more viewers.

BEST PRACTICESFor Creating Unique Keywords

Imagine yourself as a reader. Think about the words and phrases potential readers might search for when they are looking for books similar to yours. Think about yourself as the reader and think of keywords that are relevant.

Utilize long-tail keywords: Long-tail keywords are more precise phrases that are able to in attracting a certain target audience. As an example instead of using the generic word "mystery," you might make use of "cozy mysteries set in a tiny town."

Utilize all the available keywords slots available: Amazon lets you use maximum seven keywords therefore, make the most of each of them. Do not repeat keywords, or fill up space by using irrelevant terms.

Avoid overly broad or vague words: Terms like "fiction" and "romance" are not specific enough and aren't going to help your novel make a mark in an overcrowded market. Instead, you should use more precise words that define your book.

Utilize tools to create keywords. There are a variety of online tools, both paid and free, which can assist you in creating keywords that are based on the book's subject matter, theme and themes. A few of the most well-known options are Publisher Rocket, KDP Rocket as well as Google AdWords.

Use keywords that are pertinent to the book you are writing: Do not try to convince readers to clicking through your book employing irrelevant or misguided terms. This can lead to poor reviews and a loss of sales.

Change and update your keywords frequently Be aware of your book's sales and performance and make adjustments to your keyword phrases as required. Test different keywords, and eliminate the less-performing keywords, and remain willing to experiment and improve your book's visibility.

Chapter 5: Reaching Your Target Audience

The right categories to choose to your book will aid in reaching your intended readership. When you choose categories that you think your reader will appreciate it is possible to ensure that your book will be targeted to the correct individuals. This will to increase the likelihood of the book being bought and read by the people who will most likely take pleasure in the book.

Improved sales ranking

Amazon's sales ranks are tightly linked to the categories that the book is placed under. When a book does very well within a specific area, it will improve its position within the area. In turn, the book could appear more prominent on search results, which makes it more noticeable to prospective viewers. When you choose the best areas for your book it will increase the chances to rank well, and eventually boost sale.

Gaining confidence

Selecting the appropriate categories to your book will increase your credibility for your work as an author. If you choose subjects that relate to the book you're writing, it indicates that you've got a solid knowledge of the audience you want to reach and also that you've conducted the necessary study. It can to build trust with readers as well as establish yourself as a reputable authority within the field you're in.

Making yourself stand out from the crowd

If you select areas that aren't as than competitive, you will improve the odds of your book being noticed from the rest of the books. If your book is placed within highly competitive categories you could get obscured by other titles. If you select areas that aren't as crowded yet still relevant to the content of your book, you will increase the likelihood of having your book read by readers who might be interested in reading it.

Selecting the appropriate category for your book is important for getting your message to the right audience and boosting sales as well as establishing credibility and distinguishing yourself from other books. Be sure to conduct your homework and pick the categories that match your work and can aid you in achieving your objectives as an writer. By choosing the appropriate category, you will boost the visibility of your book and eventually achieve greater popularity.

Uploading your files

If you are publishing your book through Amazon's KDP platform one important step is to upload your book's files.

Correctly uploading your file is crucial to ensure the book's formatting properly, appears professional and doesn't contain any mistakes. In this section I'll talk about how important it is to upload your book's files in a correct manner to your Amazon KDP platform.

Ensuring proper formatting

Making sure that your book is uploaded correctly is essential to ensure that the book has been formatted in a correct manner. Errors in formatting could create a look that is not professional and make it hard to understand. When you upload your file correct, you'll be sure that the book has been designed the way you want to format it and it appears professional.

Beware of mistakes

Making sure your file is uploaded correctly will assist you in avoiding mistakes in your manuscript. If you upload your file that contains mistakes, these errors could appear in the finished product. The result could be negative reviews, less sales and even a tarnished reputation as an author. When you upload your files properly You can spot mistakes prior to them making it to the finished product. You can also make sure that the book you are writing is free of errors.

Accelerating the review process

Correctly uploading your file can assist in speeding the process of reviewing. In the event that you upload file in a wrong or incorrect way, this could cause delays in the process of reviewing which could mean it takes longer to get approval to be published. If you upload your files properly will ensure your review goes without a hitch and your book gets completed as swiftly as is possible.

Achieving a positive reader experience

Making sure your files are uploaded correctly is crucial to ensure an enjoyable experience for readers. If your publication is difficult to read, contains mistakes in formatting, or contains a large number of errors, the readers could suffer a bad experience and write negative review. If you upload your documents in a proper manner, you can be sure that your work is simple to read, professional looking and creates a great user experience.

Copyright protection for your business

In the end, transferring the files in a proper manner is crucial in protecting your copyright when you are an author. When you upload content which isn't your original creation or infringes on someone who owns the copyright, it may create legal issues and harm your image for being an author. When you upload your files properly and being sure that you've got all the rights to what that you publish, you'll be able to ensure your copyright is protected and avoid legal problems.

When it comes to uploading your documents correctly is vital to ensure proper formatting to avoid errors, expediting the review process as well as providing an excellent reading experience for the reader, as well as safeguarding your copyright. Be sure to adhere to the instructions set out by Amazon and check your file prior to uploading them, so that your book is professional and doesn't contain error. If you upload your files correctly it is possible to publish an excellent book and enjoy the success you desire being an author.

Best Practices

To upload your files for uploading to Amazon KDP:

Make sure you have a professional-looking cover. Your book's cover will be the very first image that readers will see. Therefore, ensure that it is appealing and professional. Don't use images that aren't high-quality or texts that are difficult to comprehend.

Pick the correct format for your file: Amazon KDP accepts several formats for files, such as Microsoft Word, PDF, as well as HTML. Select the one which best meets your requirements and be sure your data is formatted correctly and free from mistakes.

Utilizing the right formatting formatting could make a huge improvement in the accessibility of your publication. Utilize the same fonts and styles with proper spacing and make sure that the text is properly aligned.

Make sure to check your file for mistakes before uploading it be sure you have be sure to proofread your document thoroughly for any errors in grammar, spelling and punctuation. Use software such as Grammarly or seek the assistance from a professional editor.

Create a table of contents An organized table of contents can assist users navigate through your book efficiently. Be sure to include chapters' titles as well as page numbers.

Utilize high-quality photos: If the book contains images be sure that they're top-quality and formatted correctly. Don't use images with low resolution or images protected by copyright.

Use Amazon's guidelines to guide you: Amazon has specific guidelines on book format and contents. Be sure to study and adhere to these rules in order for ensuring your book gets approved for publication.

Try your book on a variety of devices: Before you publish your book, ensure that you test your book on various devices, like an Kindle or iPad for a better understanding of how the book looks and works properly.

If you follow these guidelines You can be sure that your book is properly formatted free of errors and attractive to potential readers improving your chances of success Amazon KDP.

Reviewing your book

If you are publishing your book through Amazon's KDP platform one essential step is to preview your book prior to making it available for publication. A preview of your book lets readers to examine the layout, format and contents prior to the time the book goes live on Amazon. This chapter will go over why it's important to take time to fully review your book's layout, formatting and content in Amazon KDP before submitting your book.

Ensuring proper formatting

Preparing your book for publication it's crucial to make sure you have the correct formatting. When you preview your book and examining it, you will be able to verify whether the font, images and layout are exactly as they were intended to look. It is also possible to ensure the tables of contents and page numbers are accurate and your book is professional looking and well-polished. Making sure you catch any formatting mistakes before your book's launch on Amazon could help you avoid bad reviews as well as potential problems for readers.

Checking for errors

The process of previewing your work prior to publishing is essential in identifying the errors. Although you've already proofread your manuscript multiple times, there might some errors that fall between the lines. When you preview your book on Amazon KDP You can detect errors regarding spelling, grammar and punctuation. Finding these issues before the book is released can avoid negative reviews as well as a poor reputation for the author.

Verifying that the content is true

The process of previewing your book prior to publication is essential to make sure that the content you write about is accurate. Through a thorough review of your book's contents it is possible to make sure that the book is organized and simple to read. Also, you can ensure that the book's content is concise and the information that you're providing is correct. Making sure you catch any content mistakes before the book is published can to avoid bad reviews and possible difficulties with potential readers.

Last-minute adjustments

The option to preview your book through Amazon KDP will also permit the author to make any last minute changes. If you discover any error or format issue when you are previewing your book, you'll be able to edit the cover or manuscript prior to when your book launches. It can save you from any need to update your book after publication, which could be lengthy and difficult to handle.

Chapter 6: Achieving A Positive Reader Experience

The final step is to preview your novel in Amazon KDP is vital to offering a pleasant reading experience. In ensuring that your book is formatted correctly in addition to catching any errors, as well as checking that your content is in order it will offer a top-quality user experience. This will result in favorable reviews, increased sales and an excellent reputation as an writer.

To conclude making the effort to fully preview your work in Amazon KDP before publishing is vital to make sure that your book is formatted correctly as well as identifying any mistakes, making sure the accuracy of the text as well as making changes at the last minute as well as providing the best possible reading experience for the reader. Review the layout, format and contents prior to posting it to Amazon. By examining your book thoroughly it is possible to publish an excellent book and enjoy the success you desire in your career as an author.

THE BEST PRACTICES

You can preview your book by using Amazon KDP:

Take the time to review the preview thoroughly After you've published your book and the preview has been produced, you should take time to take the time to thoroughly review it. It is your chance to ensure that your book is exactly as you'd like before the publication date.

Verify the formatting Check the formatting: One of the foremost things you should check when you preview your book is the layout of your manuscript. Be sure there aren't any errors or inconsistencies such as the spacing of your book, size and font or indentation of paragraphs.

Find any mistakes Also, go through your work to find any grammar or spelling mistakes. Utilize the preview feature to spot any errors you might miss while editing.

Examine the table of content The table of contents in your book is important. an index ensure that it's accurate and formatted in a correct manner.

Examine the links Check the hyperlinks: If your publication contains or contains links such as links to external websites, or different parts within the text, you should test your book's preview in order to ensure they function in a correct manner.

Make sure to check the cover. Make sure to look over the cover of your book as well. Check that the cover looks nice and is of the proper dimensions and resolution.

Preview across different gadgets: Amazon KDP allows you to view your book's preview across a wide range of devices. This includes Kindle electronic readers, Fire tablets, and the Kindle app. You should check out your book across as many devices as feasible to make sure it appears good on all of the devices.

Request feedback: If it is possible Get feedback from other authors regarding the first look of your novel. Request beta readers and others authors to share their opinions about the format the cover and appearance of your book.

If you follow these "best methods" to preview your manuscript by using Amazon KDP You can make sure that your book appears great and is ready to go out.

ROYALTIES

If you're a self-published writer who has selected Amazon KDP as your publishing platform, it's important to be aware of how royalties are calculated. In this post

I'll go over the meaning of royalty and how they're determined on Amazon KDP.

What is Royalties?

The term "royalty" refers to the amount authors get for sale of their book. When self-publishing via Amazon KDP the author has the option of setting the price of your book and pick from two different royalty rates that are 35% or 70 70%.

How do I set up royalties through Amazon KDP?

For setting up royalties through Amazon KDP to set up royalties on KDP, you'll be required to log in to your account. Then, select the book you would like to establish royalties for. Then, you will be able to select the royalty option you want to use and choose your price list. Additionally, you will be required to enter your payment details so Amazon can transfer your royalty to your account.

What is the formula for calculating royalties?

Royalties paid on Amazon KDP are determined based on the listed prices of your book as well as the option of royalty you've selected. If you select the option of 35% royalty the royalty amount is determined by subtracting cost of printing, shipping charges, and an unadjusted fee from the cost of the book. The remainder will become your royalty payout.

If you select the option of 70% royalty the royalty you pay is determined by subtracting expenses for printing, transport as well as a fixed cost from the cost of the book. Additionally, Amazon will deduct a delivery cost based on dimensions of your book's files. The balance will then be the royalty amount you pay.

It's important to keep in mind that Amazon can also subtract the applicable tax from the royalty you receive.

Knowing how royalty payments work in Amazon KDP is crucial for self-published authors. If you set up your royalty appropriately, you can be sure that you are receiving the correct payment for the work that you put in. Remember the fact that Amazon KDP offers two royalty options: 35% or 70%. Additionally, royalty rates are calculated according to the cost of your book as well as the shipping costs associated with the chosen choice. Setting up the right royalty rates is a crucial step in the process of self-publishing and will make sure you succeed as an author Amazon KDP.

PRICING BOOKS

If you are a self-published writer through Amazon KDP making the best price for your work can have a major impact on the number of books sold and how much revenue you earn. In this section of my book, I'll discuss some of the aspects to take into consideration in deciding on a price to sell your work on Amazon KDP.

Market Research

Before determining the price of your book's price for publication on Amazon KDP, it is essential to perform market study. It involves analyzing the costs of comparable books within your field and studying the sales performance of their books. It is also important to think about the audience you want to reach with the book as well as their purchasing behavior.

Production Costs

A different aspect to take into consideration when deciding the cost of your book Amazon KDP is the creation cost. It includes costs for formatting, editing, as well as cover design. The key is to include these expenses into your pricing plan so that you can ensure that you're earning a profit.

Royalty Options

Amazon KDP offers two royalty choices for authors who self-publish that are 35% and 70 percent. The option of 35% royalty can be found for books with a price between $0.99 to $2.98 and the 70% option is only available to book prices between $2.99 to $9.99. Consider these options of royalty when choosing an appropriate price for your novel.

Marketing Strategy

The marketing plan you choose to implement can affect the cost of the book you publish in Amazon KDP. If you are planning to run an advertising campaign or providing discounts, it is important consider these factors into the pricing plan.

The right price to sell the book you publish to publish on Amazon KDP is a vital part of self-publishing. Considerations to take into account include research on the market along with production costs, royalties choices, and a strategy for marketing. When you take a close look at these aspects and options, you will be able to determine a price that maximizes the amount of sales and profits and still cover your expenses for production. Be aware that determining the best price for your publication isn't a decision that can be made in one go and requires constant review and adjustment in response to the market and on feedback from customers.

Best Practices

Setting a Fair Price for the book

Find out the marketplace by looking at other books within your particular genre or area and see what the prices are. Take a look at traditional published books and self-published ones for a better understanding of what people are willing to shell out for comparable books.

Think about the costs of production Consider how much it costs to produce your book. This includes the design of your cover, editing and formatting. The goal is to determine an amount that will cover the costs of production and permits you to revenue.

Set goals that are in balance: Take a look at your objectives for the book. Do you wish to turn a money and are you interested in getting your work into the hands of people who want to read it? According to your objectives it is possible modify your pricing strategies in line with your goals.

Explore different pricing options Be open to play around with various pricing points to find out which one is the most effective for your work. Try pricing your book more or less and even offer promotions or discounts to see how people react.

Keep track of sales and make adjustments when necessary Be aware of the sales of your book and modify the price strategy as required. If the book you're selling isn't performing in a satisfactory manner, you might need reduce the price or employ a different approach to marketing. In contrast If your book is being sold it is possible to look at raising the cost in order to increase your profit.

SPREENING YOUR BOOK

Self-publishing with Amazon KDP could be an excellent way to promote your book however, how do promote it after you've published it? In this article I'll discuss methods to market your book that you self-published via Amazon KDP.

Utilize Amazon KDP Tools:

Amazon KDP offers a variety of tools that promote self-published authors improve their exposure and sell more books. They include Kindle Countdown Deals, Free Book Promotions, and Amazon Advertising. Making use of these tools will aid in bringing your book to an even larger audience.

Create an Author Platform

Establishing an author's online platform is crucial to promote the self-published work you've written. It involves developing a site for the author as well as social media profiles, and email lists that allow you to interact with your readers as well as promote your work. Engagement and consistency are the key for building a solid author's platform.

Review reviews:

Review reviews are an effective method for marketing your self-published work via Amazon KDP. The positive reviews will increase your book's popularity and trustworthiness. It is possible to solicit reviews from family members, friends, and authors from your field, as well in book blogs and review websites for books.

Engage Your Audience

Engaging your readers is essential to build an engaged readership as well as marketing your self-published book through Amazon KDP. It could include replying to reviews from readers and feedback, hosting competitions or giveaways, and engaging with your readers via social websites.

Collaboration with other authors:

Collaboration with authors from your niche can help get new readers to your book and also advertise your book that you self-published via Amazon KDP. It could include co-writing an ebook, participating in promotions, giveaways, or joint events and even guest blogging on other websites.

To conclude, the process of marketing your book that you self-published through Amazon KDP necessitates a systematic plan that involves the use of Amazon KDP resources, developing an author website, soliciting reviews, sharing your book with an customers, and joining forces with authors. Keep in mind that book promotion is an ongoing process which demands consistent effort as well as participation. It is possible to increase your book's exposure and reach a wider crowd through Amazon KDP by taking the time to effectively promote your book.

Chapter 7: Social Media Marketing

Self-publishing your book can be challenging, but blogging, social media, as well as email lists are efficient tools in getting public to know about your book. In this essay I'll go over how you can utilize these tools efficiently to promote your book.

Social Media

Social media sites such as Facebook, Twitter, Instagram as well as LinkedIn are excellent places to advertise your novel. Here are a few tips on how to use social media in marketing your novel:

Create an profile page for your author to post information about updates, sneak peeks as well as promotions for your novel.

Make use of hashtags to make it simpler for your readers to discover your content. Think about using hashtags specifically related to the genre of your book like #romancebooks, or mysterythriller.

Engage your readers in response to messages and posts. This will help you create a an audience of people who care about your job.

Collaborate with fellow authors and book bloggers to participate in blogs tours, or even social media takesovers.

Blogs

Blogs are a fantastic opportunity to gain an audience as well as advertise your book. Here are a few tips on marketing your book:

Make a blog relating to your novel's genre or the subject. This will help you to attract readers who are attracted by the topic.

Write guest posts on other websites related to your niche or topic. It will help you get more readers and develop connections with bloggers.

Offer exclusive content, or sneak peeks of your blog posts to motivate users to check out your blog.

You can host giveaways and contests on your blog to entice readers to take part in your blog posts.

Email Lists

Lists of emails are an effective instrument for promoting your work to people who have expressed interest in your book. Here are some suggestions on how to use emails to promote your novel:

Create an email address using a tool such as Mailchimp as well as ConvertKit.

Give a free trial chapter, or any other exclusive material to entice readers to join your email newsletter.

Regularly send out newsletters that contain news about the book's development along with exclusive content and special offers.

Offer promotions or discounts exclusive to your email subscribers in order to convince customers to buy the book.

Conclusion: Social media, blogs, as well as emails can be effective methods for promoting the self-published work you've written. Through creating an author page, interacting with readers, creating guest blogs, publishing exclusive content by using email lists you'll be able to build an web presence and draw attention interested in your work. Utilizing the tools you have at hand it is possible to boost the visibility of your book and gain the success of a self-published writer.

BEST PRACTICESFor Creating Unique Keywords

Consider yourself a reader in the same way: Take note of the terms or phrases potential readers might search for when they are looking for books similar to your own. Think about yourself in their shoes and create a list of appropriate keywords.

Make use of long-tail keywords. Long-tail keywords are specialized phrases that are able to in attracting a certain market. In this case instead of broad terms like "mystery," you might choose to use "cozy cozy mystery in a small town."

Utilize all the available keywords slots available: Amazon permits you to use as many as seven keywords, therefore, make the most of each of them. Avoid repetition of keywords and wasting space by using irrelevant terms.

Avoid ambiguous or broad phrases: Keywords such as "fiction" as well as "romance" are not specific enough and aren't going to help your novel make a mark in an overcrowded market. Instead, choose precise terms that define your book.

Utilize tools to create keywords. There are a variety of different tools for sale, both free and paid which can assist you in creating keywords for your book based on its subject matter, theme and themes. A few of the most well-known options are Publisher Rocket, KDP Rocket and Google AdWords.

Make sure that your keywords are relevant to the book you are writing: Do not try to trick people to buy your ebook by utilizing irrelevant or confusing words. It will result in bad reviews and possibly lost sales.

Change and update your keyword list regularly keep an eye on the book's sales as well as its the performance of your search results, and then adjust the keywords you use as necessary. Test the latest keywords, eliminate underperforming keywords, and remain willing to experiment and improve your book's visibility.

Selecting the right category

If you decide to publish your book via Amazon's KDP platform One of the primary aspects you have to consider is select the category your book will be placed under. Selecting the correct categories could significantly impact the visibility and popularity of your book. In this article I'll go over the importance of selecting good topics for your book KDP.

Increasing discoverability

The right category to your book will aid users to find your book. Amazon's search algorithm makes use of categories to arrange and rank results from searches. If you select relevant categories for your book, you will improve the odds of being found in search results relevant to your book and increase its visibility overall.

Reaching your target audience

The right categories to choose to your book will assist you in reaching your ideal readers. If you select categories you think your reader will like You can be sure that your book will be targeted to the correct audience. This could improve the odds that your book will be purchased and read by people who will most likely take pleasure in the content.

Improved sales ranking

The sales ranking of Amazon is closely dependent on the category which a book's listing is. If a book is able to sell successfully in a certain subject, it may boost its standing within that particular category. This means that it may be ranked higher on search results, which makes it more accessible to future viewers. If you select the appropriate areas for your book you will improve the odds to rank well, and eventually improve its book's sales.

Gaining confidence

Selecting the appropriate categories to your book will increase your credibility for your work as a writer. When you pick the right categories for the book you're writing, it implies that you've got a solid comprehension of your audience and also that you've conducted the necessary study. This will help you to build trust with readers as well as establish yourself as an expert in the field you're in.

Differentiating yourself from other competitors

If you select subjects that are not as than competitive, you will boost the likelihood of your book being noticed in the midst of the pack. If your book is placed within highly competitive categories it could be obscured by other titles. If you select the categories that are less popular however still pertinent to the book you will increase the likelihood of having your book read by prospective readers.

Selecting the appropriate category for your book is important for getting your message to the right audience and boosting sales as well as establishing credibility and distinguishing yourself from other books. Do the research you need to do and choose the categories that match your work and can aid you in achieving your objectives as an writer. By choosing the appropriate category, you will boost the visibility of your book and, ultimately, achieve more success.

Uploading your files

In publishing a book using Amazon's KDP platform one crucial step is uploading the book's file. Making sure that your book files are uploaded correctly is vital to make sure that your book has been formatted properly, appears professional and free of mistakes. In this section I'll talk about how important it is to upload your book's files in a correct manner to Amazon KDP. Amazon KDP platform.

Ensuring proper formatting

Making sure that your book is uploaded correctly is essential to ensure that the book has been formatted properly. Errors in formatting could cause your book to look unprofessional and can make it hard to be read. If you upload your documents correct, you'll be sure your book's formatting is in the manner you wanted it to look and it appears professional.

Beware of mistakes

Correctly uploading your files can assist you in avoiding mistakes within your work. If you upload a file containing imperfections, the errors will appear within the final version. It could result in bad reviews, less sales as well as a negative reputation for an author. When you upload your files properly You can spot mistakes prior to them making it into your final book and assure that your work is free of errors.

Review process speeding up

Making sure your files are uploaded correctly will aid in speeding up the process of reviewing. In the event that you upload documents incorrectly, or with the incorrect format, it could delay the review process and could take longer to be accepted to be published. If you upload your files properly will ensure the process of reviewing goes as smoothly and your book gets released as fast as it can be.

Giving readers a great experience

Making sure your files are uploaded correctly is crucial to ensure an enjoyable experience for readers. If your book is hard to read, contains mistakes in formatting, or has a lot of errors, the readers could suffer a bad experience and even leave bad review. If you upload your documents in a proper manner, you can be sure that your work is simple to read, professional looking and creates a great reader experience to your readers.

How to protect your copyright

In the end uploading your files in a safe and secure manner is crucial to protect the copyright rights of an author. If you upload a document that's not your own work, or violates anyone who owns the copyright, it may cause legal problems and affect your credibility for being an author. When you upload your files properly and making sure you own all the rights to the information you're releasing, you'll ensure your copyright is protected and avoid legal problems.

When it comes to uploading the correct files is crucial for the correct formatting and avoidance of errors, speeding the process of reviewing, ensuring the best experience to readers and securing your copyright. Be sure to adhere to the directions that are provided by Amazon and examine your documents prior to uploading them, so that your book is professional and free of mistakes. If you upload your files correctly then you will be able to create an excellent book and enjoy your goals in your career as an author.

THE BEST PRACTICES

To upload your files on Amazon KDP:

Make sure you have a professional-looking cover. Your book's cover will be the very first image that readers are likely to see. So be sure that your cover is appealing and professional. Don't use images that aren't high-quality or texts that are difficult to understand.

Pick the correct type of file: Amazon KDP accepts several types of file formats like Microsoft Word, PDF, as well as HTML. Select the one most suitable for your needs and be sure your data is formatted correctly and free from mistakes.

Make sure you use the correct formatting. Proper formatting could make a huge impact on the reading quality of your work. Utilize the same fonts and sizes with proper spacing and make sure that the text is properly aligned.

Verify your file for any errors Prior to uploading your file be sure you have be sure to proofread your document thoroughly for any errors regarding spelling, grammar and punctuation. Use software such as Grammarly or enlist the aid of an experienced editor.

Create a table of contents An organized table of contents can assist readers to navigate the book efficiently. Be sure to include the chapter title and page number.

Utilize high-quality photos: If you have images in your book be sure that they're top-quality and formatted correctly. Do not use low-resolution or images protected by copyright.

Use Amazon's guidelines to guide you: Amazon has specific guidelines on book format and contents. You must read and adhere to these rules in order for ensuring your book gets approved for publication.

Try your book out on different devices: Before you publish your book, ensure to test it on various devices, like an Kindle or iPad for a better understanding of how it functions and looks good.

When you adhere to these top practices You can be sure that your work is formatted properly with no errors, as well as appealing to potential readers improving your odds of a successful launch with Amazon KDP.

REVIEWING BOOKS

If you are publishing your book through Amazon's KDP platform one crucial step is preparing your book for preview before making it available for publication. A preview of your book lets the reader to check out the layout, format as well as the content prior to when it is published on Amazon. This chapter will talk about how important it is to take the time to fully review your book's layout, formatting and content in Amazon KDP prior to making it available for publishing.

Ensuring proper formatting

Preparing your book for publication it's essential to ensure an appropriate formatting. When you preview your book and examining it, you will be able to verify that your images, font and layout of your book are what you wanted them to look. It is also possible to ensure that your tables of contents and page numbers are accurate as well as that the book is professional looking and well-polished. Making sure you catch any formatting mistakes prior to publishing your book on Amazon will help avoid negative reviews as well as potential problems for readers.

Checking for errors

The process of previewing your work prior to publishing is crucial in catching mistakes. Although you've already proofread your book several times, there might mistakes that get into the gaps.

When you preview your book on Amazon KDP it is possible to spot mistakes that are grammatical, spelling and punctuation. Making sure you catch these mistakes before your publication is published can to avoid bad reviews and poor reputation for the author.

Making sure the information is accurate

The process of previewing your book prior to publication is essential to ensure that the content you write about is accurate. When you review the content of your book it is possible to make sure that the book is organized and easy to navigate. It is also possible to ensure the message of your book is concise and your information is correct. Finding any errors in the content before your publication goes online can to avoid bad reviews and possible difficulties with customers.

Last-minute adjustments

The option to preview your book through Amazon KDP can also allow the author to make any last minute changes. If you discover any error or format issue when you are previewing your manuscript, you are able to modify your cover file or the manuscript before the book is released. This will help avoid any need to update your book after the book has been published which could be lengthy and stressful.

Giving readers a great experience

The final step is to preview your novel in Amazon KDP is vital to offering a pleasant reading experience. In ensuring that your book is formatted correctly as well as catching any errors as well as ensuring that the content is accurate and accurate, you will be able to give a superior reader experience to your readers. This will result in favorable reviews, increased sales and an excellent reputation as an writer.

As a final note it is important to fully preview your work through Amazon KDP before publishing is vital to make sure that your book is formatted correctly in addition to identifying any errors and making sure the accuracy of the text as well as making changes at the last minute as well as providing the best possible reading experience for the reader. Review the layout, format and contents prior to posting it to Amazon. If you have a clear preview of your book it is possible to publish an excellent book and enjoy the success you desire being an author.

Best Practices

You can preview your book by using Amazon KDP:

Examine the preview with care After you've put up your book's files and the preview created, make sure you take the time to review the preview carefully. This is the chance to ensure that the book appears exactly how you would like it to look prior to publication.

Make sure the formatting is correct The foremost things you should check when you preview your book is the format of the book. Check to ensure that there aren't any mistakes or omissions, for example space, font sizes or the indentation of paragraphs.

Check for any errors Also, examine your manuscript for grammar or spelling errors. Make use of the preview to identify any errors that you could not have noticed in the process of editing.

Review the table of contents In the event that your book has a the table of contents ensure that the format is correct and written properly.

Examine the hyperlinks Check the hyperlinks: If your publication contains hyperlinks, for example hyperlinks to external sites or different parts within the text, you should test these in the preview section to verify that they are working in a correct manner.

Examine the cover: Make sure to look over the cover of your book as well. Check that the cover looks great and has the right dimension and resolution.

Preview across different device: Amazon KDP allows you to read your book in preview using a range of different devices, such as Kindle electronic readers, Fire tablets, and the Kindle app. Make sure you review your work across as many devices as feasible to make sure the book looks great on all of the devices.

Ask for feedback: If you can seek feedback from your readers regarding the first look of your novel. Get feedback from beta readers, or ask other authors for feedback regarding the layout as well as the overall appearance of your book.

If you follow these "best methods" when previewing your work by using Amazon KDP If you follow these "best practices," you will make sure that your book appears great and is ready for publication.

ROYALTIES

If you're self-published author and have chosen Amazon KDP as your publishing platform, it's important to be aware of how royalties are calculated. In this post I'll explain the nature of royalties and how they're calculated using Amazon KDP.

What are Royalties?

The term "royalty" refers to the amount an author gets for sale of their book. If you self-publish your book through Amazon KDP the author has the option of setting the price of your book and select among two options for royalty that are 35% or 70 percent.

How can I setup the Royalties for Amazon KDP?

In order to set up royalty payments via Amazon KDP You will be required to log in to your account. Then, choose the book that you wish to create royalties on. There, you'll be able to choose your preferred royalty rate and then set the price of your list. Also, you'll be required to enter your payment details so Amazon will transfer your royalty to your account.

What is the formula for calculating royalties?

The royalties charged by Amazon KDP are calculated using the list cost of your book, as well as the option of royalty you've selected. If you select the 35% royalty rate Your royalty is determined by subtracting printing expenses, shipping charges as well as a fixed cost from the cost of the book. The rest will be your royalty payout.

If you select the option of 70% royalty Your royalty is determined by subtracting expenses for printing, transport as well as a fixed cost from the cost of the book. Additionally, Amazon will deduct a delivery cost based on size of the book's file. The balance will then be the royalty amount you pay.

It's important to keep in mind that Amazon will deduct any the applicable tax from your royalty payout.

Understanding how royalties function on Amazon KDP is crucial for self-published authors. When you arrange your royalties appropriately, you will be sure you will receive an appropriate amount of compensation for the hard work you put into it. You must remember you have two options for royalty. Amazon KDP offers two royalty options: 35% or 70%. Additionally, royalty rates are based on the price you list for your book as well as the shipping charges associated with each choice. Setting up the right royalty rates is a crucial step in the process of self-publishing. It can make sure you succeed as an author with Amazon KDP.

THE PRICE YOU BOOK

If you are a self-published writer using Amazon KDP making the best price for your book could significantly impact the amount of sales you make and your revenue. In this part of my book, I'll go over what factors you should consider in deciding on a price to sell your book Amazon KDP.

Market Research

Prior to deciding on a price for your book's price to be sold on Amazon KDP, it is essential to perform market study. This includes looking at price of books similar to the same genre, and then analyzing their performance in sales. It is also important to think about the audience you want to reach with the book as well as their purchasing behavior.

Cost of Production

A different aspect to take into consideration in deciding on the price of the book you publish on Amazon KDP is the creation cost. It includes costs for editing, formatting, as well as designing the cover. The key is to include the cost of these items in your pricing strategies so that you can ensure that you're profitable.

Royalty Options

Amazon KDP offers two royalty choices for authors who self-publish that are 35% and 70 percent. The 35% option can be found for books with a price between $0.99 to $2.98 The 70% option is only available to books that cost between $2.99 to $9.99. You should take into consideration these options of royalty when choosing the price of your novel.

Marketing Strategy

The marketing plan you choose to implement can influence the cost of your book Amazon KDP. If you are planning to run promotions or giving discounts, it is important include these in the pricing strategy.

The right price to sell the book you publish publishing on Amazon KDP is an important part of self-publishing. Considerations to take into account include research into the market and production costs, as well as royalty choices, and a strategy for marketing. When you be attentive to these elements to set the price that maximizes your revenue and sales and still cover your expenses for production. Make sure you set the correct price for your publication will not be a single-time choice and requires constant review and adjusting based upon developments in the marketplace and comments from clients.

THE BEST ACTIVITIES

Setting a Fair Price for the book

Find out the marketplace and look up other titles within your particular genre or area and see what the prices are. Take a look at traditional and self-published titles for a better understanding of the prices that readers can expect to pay for similar titles.

Think about the costs of production Consider how much it costs to produce your book. This includes the design of your cover, editing and formatting. It is important to establish an amount that will cover the costs of production and permits the book to earn a income.

Set goals that are in balance: Take a look at your objectives for the book. Are you looking to earn profits and are you focused on getting your work into the hands of potential readers? The answer depends on what you want to achieve it is possible modify your pricing strategies in line with your goals.

Explore different pricing options Be open to play around with various prices to determine which one is the most effective for your work. It is possible to price your book either higher or lower and even offer discounts or other promotions to see what readers think of it.

Keep track of sales and make adjustments when necessary Be aware of the book's sales, and alter the pricing strategy if needed. If the book you're selling isn't performing effectively, it may be necessary to reduce your cost or consider a new approach to marketing. In contrast

If your book is selling very well it is possible to look at raising the cost for maximum profits.

Promoting your book

Self-publishing your book on Amazon KDP is an excellent way to make your book known however, how do promote it after the book is published? In this article I'll explore strategies to advertise the self-published book you've created through Amazon KDP.

Utilize Amazon KDP Tools:

Amazon KDP offers a variety of promotional tools that can help self-published authors boost exposure and sell more books. They include Kindle Countdown Deals, Free Book Promotions, and Amazon Advertising. Making use of these tools will assist in reaching more people.

Develop an Author Platform

Establishing an author's online platform is crucial to promote your book that you self-published. This requires the creation of a website for your author and social media accounts and email lists that allow you to interact with your readers as well as promote your work. Inconsistency and interaction are essential in building an effective author profile.

Review reviews:

Reviews can be a very effective tool to promote your self-published novel through Amazon KDP. The positive reviews will increase the visibility of your book and increase its credibility. It is possible to solicit reviews from family members, friends, and authors from your field, as well with book bloggers and review websites for books.

Connect with your Audience:

Engaging your readers is essential to build an engaged readership as well as advertising your self-published work on Amazon KDP. It can involve responding to the comments and reviews of readers organizing contests, giveaways, and giveaways as well as engaging with your users on social networks.

Work with Other Authors to:

Collaboration with authors from your field can allow you to get new readers to your book and also market your self-published work via Amazon KDP. It could include co-writing the book, taking part in giveaways or promotions jointly and even guest blogging on the websites of each other.

The final word is that advertising your self-published work via Amazon KDP is a must. You need a well-planned approach that incorporates making use of Amazon KDP sources, establishing an author's platform, soliciting reviews, engaging to your readership, as well as working with authors. Be aware that book marketing is a continuous process that demands consistent effort and involvement. It is possible to increase your book's popularity and draw a bigger crowd through Amazon KDP by taking the time to effectively promote your book.

SOCIAL MEDIA Marketing

The marketing of your self-published book may be difficult, however blogs, social media as well as email lists are effective tools to get the message out about your work. In this article I'll go over how to make use of these tools in order to advertise your book.

Social Media

Social media websites such as Facebook, Twitter, Instagram as well as LinkedIn can be excellent places for promoting your work. Here are some suggestions for making use of social media for marketing your novel:

Create an author page or profile that allows you to post updates, sneak peaks as well as promotions associated with the book you wrote.

Utilize hashtags in order to make it easier for your readers to locate your content. You should consider using hashtags specific to the book's genre like #romancebooks, or mysterythriller.

Be active with your fans in response to messages and posts. This will help you create a the community of followers who care about your job.

Collaboration with other book authors or bloggers to participate in blogs tours, or even social media takesovers.

Blogs

Blogs can be an excellent opportunity to gain an audience as well as help promote your book. Here are some ideas you can use to help market your book:

Make a blog in connection with your book's genre or subject. It can to attract readers who are attracted by the subject.

Create guest blog posts for other blogs that are related to your particular genre or topic. It will help you expand your reach and develop connections with bloggers.

Offer exclusive material or sneak peeks of your blog, to entice visitors to come back to your blog.

You can host giveaways and contests on your blog in order to encourage readers to take part in your posts.

Chapter 8: The Most Money Selling Kindle Ebooks

Are you interested in making cash by selling Amazon Kindle Books?

If you are, you have be more than create an eBook, then transform it into a compatible digital format, then list it on the market. This process lets you put your book up for sale in the Kindle Store However; you'd prefer to take it further. It is your goal to increase the profits you earn from Amazon Kindle Books. What do you do?

Make sure you write a quality eBook. If you write a step-by-step guide or novel ensure that your writing is of high quality.

Nobody wants to buy an unsatisfactory book. Additionally it is Amazon Kindle Store allows reviews. Amazon Kindle Store enables reviews.

If you've got a great book, it works in your favor. Contrarily an eBook that is poorly-written might get bad reviews. Negative reviews may make other customers turn away.

Make sure to proofread your book before uploading it onto Amazon's digital text platform. It is not enough to create a high-quality eBook, but also an edited one as well. If you are proofreading your book, consider your position as a person who is reading the book, not an author. Examine the text from the viewpoint of your readers. Does the narrative seem logical? Do your instructions for how-tos be clear and easy to follow? Be aware that the goal is to earn good ratings on Amazon.com. Positive reviews will increase your profits.

Write a good product description. After you've written and edited your ebook, you'll be on the journey to Amazon.com. Then, you are able to enter the platform for digital texts. First, you need to compose your description of the product. This is the only chance you have to create a lasting impression.

Write a detailed description. To provide a step-by-step guide write a summary of the subjects discussed. If you are writing a novel that is creative make an expert of every chapter, or write a summary of the narrative without providing details that are too detailed.

Preview your digital text ebook. In order to sell your ebook through Amazon's Kindle Store Amazon Kindle Store, ebooks convert to digital texts. This process is simple since Amazon manages the conversion.

But, as with all things, it may not be 100% accurate. Preview your document for formatting errors. The ebook must be easy to read with your Amazon Kindle. Your book is at risk of losing rating and low sales if problems with formatting are encountered, for instance long paragraphs.

Create a reasonable selling price. A lot of novice authors make mistakes when they are selling their book with a digital text version for Amazon's Kindle. Amazon Kindle. The error is way too expensive of a cost. Be aware that Kindle owners spent more than $300 for their device.

While it is a reasonable price for the tech used however, it's a huge amount of dollars. How can a buyer be willing to pay more than $300 only to then 20 or more dollars for each book? Do not undersell yourself, but be aware that the top-selling

Amazon Kindle books are in the between $5.99 up to $12.99.

Get people to visit you Amazon selling page. Because Amazon.com is one of the most popular websites and is the sole place to allow Kindle users to buy eligible ebooks, you'll see visitors. Your customers will be able to view your page of sales, however it doesn't mean that you cannot guide others to your site as well. Join groups for the Amazon Kindle.

Engage with the owners. Respond to questions, join discussions, and even start your own discussion. Advertise your book in all purchase, sell or trade section. Include a link to your Amazon sales pages within your signature in the event that they are permissible.

You can see that making money from selling an Amazon Kindle book involves more than writing a novel and putting it up for sale. There are a lot of electronic textbooks for purchase at Amazon.com. If you want to make the most profit you must make yourself stand out from others by using a smart approach.

Profit Maximizing With an eBook

Do you have a book or a writer who writes ebooks on hire? Do you have made your own ebook to self-publishing? If not, why would you wait to long? Writing ebooks to hire is great because you get being paid immediately for your efforts.

However you could need several months to earn the exact amount of money from an ebook that you self-publish. But, it's crucial to consider the long term. Self-published ebooks can generate residual income which means that it will continue to increase over time.

Then, how can you make the most money from an ebook that you self-published?

The first step is to look at the various options for selling. It is best to self-publish the ebook through your web page or sales site. The next choice is to make use of the self-publishing services of a third-party site like Lulu.com. In addition, you can turn your work to one of the Amazon Kindle Book.

If you are selling your self-published book through a website, this is the best option since the profits are yours to keep. There's no website that is third party that you can share earnings with.

To build a sales website you must purchase a low-cost web hosting service. An inexpensive starter plan should suffice. The domain name you choose should contain the title of your book.

When it comes to sales-related content Start with a memorable headline. Are you writing a guide ebook on working at home? If yes, then start your website with a statement like "Do you desire to avoid the long commute for work, cut down on travel costs and have more time with family? Let me demonstrate ways to work from the comfort of your own home!" Follow with the areas highlighted in the ebook or chapter outline titles. give a short excerpt as well as testimonials from customers.

For these, you can offer your free ebook via Craigslist.org to those willing to provide a quick review.

To pay for self-published eBooks through a sales website think about purchasing online shopping carts. It allows you to accept debit and credit cards. In the absence of this, you can you can accept PayPal transactions. Set the price an appropriate selling price.

The cheaper the price is, the greater number of ebooks you'll sell. Make it appear that readers are receiving a bargain. Price your eBook at $19.99 However, you can either immediately or forever cut down prices to $9.99

If you have a third-party self-publishing website such as Lulu.com It increases your reach. If you're only able to accept PayPal for payments on your sale page, consider utilizing the marketplace of a third party. They take a variety of transactions.

The result is a greater market for your product. Lulu.com permits you to make more than just ebooks. Customers can choose to purchase the printed version.

Like we said uploading your eBook on your book on the Amazon electronic text service the Amazon Kindle Book is a advantage. There is nothing to lose when you do this.

You can list your books at Amazon.com and then convert it into digital text. This is the format which is compatible with Amazon Kindle device. Amazon is paid every time the sale occurs. As per the Terms and Conditions of Amazon it amounts to 35% of fees for royalty.

For the reason to change your PDF book to Amazon's format for digital text and then upload it to sell on Amazon's Kindle Store, you've got nothing to risk. Additionally, you are targeting an audience.

It is a small, light device. Amazon Kindle is a small light device that let readers cuddle up with their favorite ebook. In some ways, it's like the Amazon Kindle has pushed ebooks into the future with no bulky computer and connect cables. Join the revolution to maximize the earnings you earn from your ebook now.

Questions to Ask When Earning Money Using Amazon The Kindle

The Amazon Kindle? Amazon Kindle?

Answer to the question: The Amazon Kindle is an electronic book reader that is also referred to by the name of an eBook reader. It weighs just under 10 ounces, the small-handled device is an easy elegant, contemporary, and convenient method to access books while on the move.

In contrast to many other devices, neither wires or computers are required. Amazon Kindles are equipped with Whispernet technology, which allows readers to download and purchase compatible books anywhere.

What is the best way to earn money using Amazon's Kindle? Amazon Kindle?

Answer: If you are an author or article writer, then you are able to benefit from this popular tool through your skills. Amazon permits authors to self-publish their work.

It is by using a specific electronic ebook format. Amazon owners can buy your ebook and install it on their devices. When this happens it earns you some money!

Do you have to pay an amount of money to sell Kindle ebooks on Amazon.com?

Answer: No. It's free to publish your self-published book on Amazon.com. The author is, in some way, charged each time an order is placed. Amazon.com manages the sales of the book, and they pay an agreed-upon royalty per sale.

Problem: How can I start?

Answer: The initial step to profit through the sales of Amazon Kindle books is to make the books. There are a lot of books that are available to purchase. For a better chance of selling, look through the available titles. Naturally, you could create ebooks with similar subjects however, unique topics and genres will yield the most money.

If you've decided you'd like to market your ebook on Amazon Kindle then you can begin creating. You can create a poetry collection or a guidebook as well as fiction or non-fiction, it is possible to write it!

It isn't it difficult to make money using Amazon Kindle Books?

Answer: It's a matter of preference. There is a huge selection of books to download and purchase. You can increase your chance of earning profits by designing an appealing cover design for your ebook, clearly describing it and offering a reasonable cost. According to the previous paragraph that books with distinctive stories or themes are more likely to be more successful, since there's more competition.

The question is: I've written an ebook to be published on Amazon Kindle and now I have to figure out how can I make it available for sale?

Answer: Go to Amazon.com. If you own an Amazon account, you can log into your account. If not, sign up for your account free of charge. After that, scroll to the bottom. There is the "Self-Publish by Us," link at the bottom.

Go to this page and visit go to the "Get Started," section of Amazon Kindle. Follow the step-by-step instructions. This involves entering your details about the product, uploading your files, as well as the setting of your price.

It is it simple to upload your media files to Amazon.com?

Answer: Yes. Simply follow their step-bystep instruction. The ebook can then be transformed into digital format. It's the technology that allows electronic reading with devices like the Amazon Kindle device. According to Amazon's site the platform supports HTML, Microsoft Word, plain text as well as Adobe PDF formats.

What is the time frame for the whole process last?

Answer: It's all in the details. The author must be aware of the amount of time required to edit and write your manuscript. After this is completed and completed, it takes only some minutes to begin the uploading process. In 12 hours in the average time the Amazon Kindle book should be accessible at Amazon.com available for purchase.

The question is how much will I make?

Answer: It's a matter of preference. The list price is what you set to sell the Amazon Kindle book. Amazon will take a portion of the price you sell. Amazon pays the seller a 35% royalty charge for every sale. What you make is contingent on the price you list as well as the number of books you've sold.

Chapter 9: Write An Ebook To Be Used On Amazon Kindle

If you are a writer who enjoys creating for enjoyment or to earn money then you should think about eBooks.

Digital books are growing in importance, yet there's a small market. Many people do not like reading books via their laptops.

According to the old saying that the majority of people want to snuggle on the couch with the best book. It's good to know that you can get them through an ebook. This is because of the invention and release of Amazon Kindle.

Amazon Kindle Amazon Kindle is a lightweight ebook reader. It weighs less than 10 grams. It is a sizeable book. it's regarded as a hybrid between a novel in paper and an hardcover book.

However, despite being similar in size this device is smaller. In case that weren't enough, it also comes with Whispernet. By using cellphone networks, users are able to wirelessly access Amazon's Amazon Kindle Book Store to shop, buy, and then upload their favourite books, magazines as well as newspapers. The technology for wireless is included as part of Kindle. Customers can purchase more ebooks in the manner they wish.

Now you're probably considering "Yes I agree that Amazon Kindle sounds like a great device, but Amazon Kindle sounds like a nice device, but what can it benefit you?" As a writer you will find it more than simply an electronic book reader it is a tool for making money.

A lot of writers are shocked to find out that Amazon.com offers self-publishing on the Kindle. The company offers. In essence, you create an ebook, set up an free Amazon.com account, go to the digital platform's website and enter the description of your book then upload and view your files, then set the selling price.

Within the next 24 hours, your eBook will appear for sale at Amazon.com on the Kindle Store.

If you've written ebooks, you're in good position. You are already familiar with how to compose ebooks, what is the ideal length and design style. It shouldn't be a problem to create an ebook on Amazon.com. It's not even necessary to create a brand new ebook.

If you've created and hold rights to an ebook You can offer it for sale through Amazon.com. Amazon.com website. You simply upload your file in the manner previously mentioned and then the site automatically transforms your file into digital text.

As you are the owner of all rights for the publication you are able to list it on Amazon's Kindle Book store, as you can continue selling the PDF edition through your site or a third-party market.

If you're an author, but you don't know how to write ebooks, you're on the right track. A lot of articles writers do not like ebooks at all costs. A lot of people are concerned about layout, length of the book and the like. The task of making an ebook might be daunting and time-consuming However, it doesn't have to be.

An ebook, in essence, is simply a compilation of information put together into a. For first-time authors, it is recommended to focus on simple topics including how-to manuals.

In the past, we have said that the best approach to ebooks is to view them as collections of information. As an example, if you plan to create an ebook about how you can make money while living happily in the current economic downturn consider writing good content for writing.

If you are a specialist in writing Web content it will be much simpler. In the introduction to your article, you will introduce the main idea of your piece, which is to make costs. Instead of writing two sentences for three sentences introduction, try making the introduction two or three paragraphs.

Within an article, every paragraph will highlight a unique aspect, like shopping with coupons in the supermarket. Instead of discussing each savings procedure in four to five paragraphs, devote a entire page discussing the topic.

When it comes to coupons, begin by explaining their value and the amount they will save the average consumer, where to locate the coupons and how to make applying coupons. After you've started writing, your word count and totals of pages quickly increase.

If you have no experience with ebooks it's best to take a take a look at how to create similar to article creating. The process is much simpler and less stressful. Essentially, you compose lengthy articles, place them in order to create a an orderly flow, and then combine these into a book.

At the end of the day, you should create the table of contents on the topic and page number. Simple as that.

For making money through Amazon.com login to your account, then go to the electronic text publishing platform where you can enter your item's description Upload your HTML text or word PDF files, initiate the conversion process, choose the price for your sale, then watch for your book to be available for purchase within Amazon's Kindle Store.

The ability to think Outside Of The Box

Do you consider yourself an article author or author who would want to increase your income? If yes, then you have to think outside the box. Instead of self-publishing an unpublished book that won't be sold or playing it safe with web-based content writing, you should take an in-depth look at Amazon Kindle.

On first look it appears that at first glance, the Amazon Kindle looks like a nice device to own. It's an electronic book reader. It's small, light and user-friendly while on the move. It is possible to consider "this is great however I prefer to write, not read."

Many writers commit the same error. Amazon.com is known for spending a significant amount of time promoting its Kindle to sell. The thing they do not shout about over the top is that it is possible to earn profits by self-publishing Kindle books.

The first step for making Amazon Kindle books is to create an ebook. The great thing about selling your book on Amazon is the fact that there are an array of subjects that you can write about. It is possible to write books on almost anything. Do you enjoy writing instructions?

Make a compilation of these and then create an ebook. Are you a fan of creative writing? If yes, let your creativity flow and begin writing.

If you're an experienced writer, or an author and author, then you are already aware of the significance of proofreading. Prior to visiting the Amazon website, it is essential to check and proofread your book.

Repeat it several time. Amazon is great in the sense that buyers can evaluate products, which includes Kindle books. But, this could work against you if the publication is strewn with mistakes. Be sure to avoid this from happening. Edit, proofread repeat the process.

While you may make a novel for sale through Amazon but you also have the opportunity to earn money off what you already own. Are you selling ebooks via your website or on third-party marketplaces?

If yes, think about it as an additional way to earn cash. Make use of the

Amazon.com site to convert your Word document into a digital version. It is possible to continue selling your eBooks through your site as well!

If you're looking to sell Amazon Kindle books, it is simple. Log into the account you have created on your Amazon account. If you're new to Amazon Create a new account for free. Scroll down until the bottom. Then, you will find a set of hyperlinks. You can click on the link called "Self-Publish With us." Then, on the next page, choose one of the options "Learn More," or "Get started."

Next, you must fill in your product's details. The details include titles, descriptions, languages the author's name, publication date keywords, and so and so on. Then, you will need an ISBN number, however it's not necessary. If you don't already have an ISBN number, you can do not bother with this step.

The next stage will be to download and transform your eBook documents to digital text. This is a breeze thanks to Amazon's digital-text platform. Use the search button to locate the file on your personal computer. It will transform HTML documents texts, text files, word documents and Adobe PDF frauds.

The last step is to determine your price for sale. When you've done this, can simply hit the button to publish. When it comes to the price for sale take your time and use your judgment. You are able to determine your price for selling, but remain careful.

Amazon gives you a 35% commission for every sale. If your pricing is too high, you might not be successful in generating revenue. However when you put your price to low, you'll not get a good return on your investment.

On average, it takes around 12 hours to get an Amazon Kindle book to appear in the Amazon website's sale. In the past, we've stated that you'll receive 35% of the royalties for every book sold. Amazon's policy states that it pays once your sales total reaches $10.

There's a chance that you don't get an immediate sale But do not let this stop you from pursuing your goals. In the meantime, you can think of the future Amazon Kindle ebook. If you write and sell several books, you will be a bestselling author, and build a base.

Chapter 10: Writing An Ebook

Are you a content writer working as a freelancer? If so, have had the chance to look over the ebooks? If not, you should.

Due to the growing popularity of the internet and electronic readers like Amazon's Amazon Kindle, writing ebooks can be a lucrative business.

If you've never published the ebook you want to publish, you might be apprehensive about writing an ebook. As a writer of web content You specialize in writing pieces that typically are around 1 page long.

In contrast an ebook may contain more than 200 pages. If you look at it from this perspective, creating the ebook may seem to be an enormous job. Consider it as writing a sequence of content. The articles are later organized in a certain order, and then compiled into a book.

How do you make an ebook?

Select the Category you want to choose from.

If you're a content writer, then you are specialized in writing informative and useful content. It is what you know best which is why you should stay to this area. If you decide take your writing further and develop into the realm of creative writing, go for it. Start by sticking with the things you're comfortable with. It will make the writing of an ebook much easier.

For the subject you choose, pick a subject that interests your personal interests, like being a parent at home or making money. You can also pick a subject which is significant for Americans like ways to reduce the effects on global warming, or how you can earn money at your home, etc.

Design a Title for Your Ebook

If you are writing a book on how-to is your goal, it's going to be simple. What do you intend to teach your viewers how to accomplish? If your goal is to save the money you spend, a great name would be "How to Organize Money in Your Wallet."

Create your Introduction

The introduction to an ebook is similar to the introduction to an article. The only difference is length. Write down the goal of your book and the motivation behind the book. Instead of condensing your intro in one paragraph, you should use the entire page.

Make Your Ebook

It's the tough portion for the majority of people. Like I said, imagine this as a set of content. First, you must create an outline. If you're looking to demonstrate your audience how you can cut costs begin by describing how you can reduce expenses. Saving money can be made for food, dining out, attire transportation, utilities etc. These can all be divided into chapters or sections.

In each chapter, you should split it up into sections. Like, for example, for saving cash at the supermarket may have one piece in which you are advised to take advantage of it, ways to help you save money, ways you can make use of coupons as well as tips on how to locate coupons and suggestions for using them to the fullest extent possible. these coupons. In a matter of minutes, you could be able to gather a selection of information that could be turned into a 10 page section or chapter.

Make Your Final Draft

The conclusion of your book should summarise the book and the information readers have got to know. Include some of the most useful and cost-saving suggestions.

Edit Your Ebook

If you're using Microsoft Word, the program helps you to catch several spelling and grammar errors. But it's not fully proofread. Therefore, you should check your manuscript and proofread it.

If you've learned the best way to create an ebook it is possible that you are wondering how to earn money off the book. It's great you've got a variety of options. Create a site and sell your eBook from there, you can also use a third party market place, such as LuLu.com to transform your book into digital format and then sell the book to customers as the Amazon Kindle book. For a better return on your investment you can do any of the three.

Websites are simple and cost-effective to design. Lulu.com as well as other marketplaces from third parties are simple to access. For the Amazon Kindle, you just have to sign up for an account that is free.

You can upload you Microsoft Word document to the digital text platform. It will convert it to digital text. This allows it to be read by Amazon Kindle customers. The book then appears on Amazon Kindle Store. Amazon Kindle Store.

Write How-To eBooks for Amazon the Kindle in just 8 easy Steps

Do you wish to benefit from the success of the Amazon Kindle? The electronic book reader is popular! It's the potential for making profits But how can you do it? There are many methods to earn money from Amazon Kindle, such as becoming a pay-per-click affiliate. If you're an author or an author on the web You can make money from the success of the Kindle with your creativity. Write an ebook, and then sell it to customers in the form of an Kindle Book.

How do you start?

Choose a category

If you want to write an ebook on how-to select a subject. It's simpler to write about interesting subjects. Discover your passion and earn money out of it. Are you a fan of building dollhouses? Make a step-by-step guide for how to build one.

By following these guides to help you the options are limitless. The most popular books teach readers to reduce costs, fight the effects of global warming, earn cash, as well as complete DIY home improvements.

Write an outline

For increased productivity and to reduce writers block, make an outline. Write it out with a pen or computer. Create the information you wish to incorporate in your book. If you're trying to demonstrate your readers how to change countertops in the kitchen the sections you write about could contain the tools needed, advice to purchase equipment, tips for preparation and replacement procedures and tips for cleaning.

Start a Word document in Microsoft Word.

Every ebook should be written by using Microsoft Word. It is a program that makes it simple to detect grammar and spelling errors as well as keep track of the word count.

Make the Introduction

The introduction to your ebook should comprise at the very least two paragraphs. Include a catchy headline. If you're writing an ebook that teaches the readers how to upgrade the countertop in their kitchen Your introduction could be something like "Are you bored of gazing at a dull, old countertop in your kitchen? Do not put off the task for too long."

Explain the purpose behind your book, which could include a guide for readers on how to upgrade their kitchen countertops. Explain how your book will help them achieve the goal. And then, say thank you to them for taking part in your journey.

Chapter 11: Pros And Cons Of Selling Amazon Kindle Ebooks

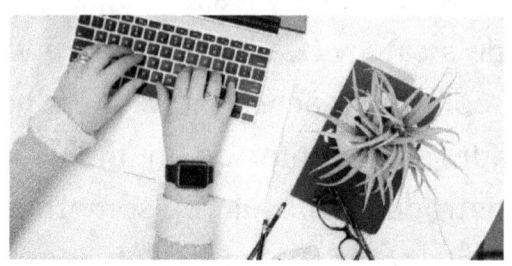

Are you a writer and is looking to earn a living? If yes, there are several choices.

Start your own blog or site and make money from your site with advertisements that are paid or submit content to websites to earn money, do jobs for hire and many more. These options are great, however you must take into consideration the possibility of writing Amazon Kindle books. If you are playing the cards correctly, it's an opportunity for making money.

Amazon Kindle Amazon Kindle is a small electronic book reader. It's sometimes referred to as the ebook reader. It's a handheld device that uses wireless technology it weighs about 10 grams.

Users are able to connect instantly directly to the Amazon Kindle Store regardless of which part of the world they reside in. There, they can purchase newspaper subscriptions as well as magazines, as well as books. If you sign up as an Kindle writer, you can ensure that your work can be uploaded on the site and then sold.

Writing and selling Amazon Kindle books is a profitable opportunity for making money. Like any other business opportunity to earn money, it comes with advantages and disadvantages. But, what exactly are they?

The whole process takes some time. Uploading your book to a website, and then turning the text into digital format is an easy process. It shouldn't take too long either. The most important thing to consider is the whole process.

The author must write your book, proofread the book, and then post the book for auction. If you're not a proficient writer who is able to rapidly process your thoughts and then type them the words, it could take many months to finish an ebook.

The way you get paid. Contrary to many third-party sites, Amazon does not technically charge a portion of the sales. Instead, they offer the seller a certain percentage. Based on their terms and conditions they pay you 35% of the royalties for every book they sell.

It's a plus that you get paid and Amazon is among the biggest marketplaces online. Therefore, your work will be viewed by a significant number of people and, hopefully, the book will sell.

It isn't a guarantee that you will sell. If you post the Amazon Kindle book for sale on the web, does not guarantee that it will get sold. It's a plus that you don't have to pay for the advertise.

In the past that you will be paid 35% of royalty payments. So, while you're not guaranteed to make the sale, there's nothing to lose taking a shot.

It is possible to breathe new fresh life into an old book. If you're the creator of an eBook or self-published publication, you own the rights to the book. That means that you are able to sell it at Amazon.com.

It is possible to continue selling either a printed book or an ebook on the internet and also sell it in Amazon Kindle format. If you have already written your book, there are zero risks. The idea is to enhance your income potential.

It's simple to convert your files to digital text. Digital text is the technology Amazon Kindle uses. It makes it simple to read books using the go with a handheld device. It's more durable than computers! Amazon.com converts your document for you. Upload your file that could be an HTML document or PDF file Text file, Word document. It will automatically cover your document.

Set your price for selling. After uploading your book to Amazon's Amazon website, you'll be asked to input an amount for selling. It is your choice to select the amount you'd like. If you self-published your book prior to this, Amazon wants you to determine a fair market price.

If you don't, you'll have full control of the cost. Remember the fact that a book that is priced too cheap will not bring in any profits, while the book that is priced excessively might not result in sales.

The book can be promoted for more revenue. In the past, Amazon.com is a popular online marketplace. Many millions of customers go to the site for shopping.

To that end, your work should receive lots of attention and visits. There are ways to help promote your book. It is possible to post your book messages on discussion boards or or write a press release about the book and then invite people to read the book.

To conclude, the writing process as well as making money selling Amazon Kindle books is a business opportunity to earn money that comes with its positives and negatives. There aren't any risks associated, besides your time, why don't you take a look at how much you could earn you?

Making money selling Amazon's Kindle ebooks Do's and Don'ts

You are an author or article writer hoping to make money from the success of Amazon Kindle? If yes, then use your writing abilities into action and make an ebook. When the ebook is finished, it can be uploaded to the Amazon site, then converted into digital format, then is sold on Amazon's Kindle Store.

In the event that you've published a book in print, an ebook, or an assortment of writings, you're in a position to benefit. Most people looking to take advantage the self-publishing option offered by Amazon are not experienced writers at all. Because of this, there are many who make errors. Unfortunately, many of those mistakes can be costly. These mistakes can lead to negative reviews, low profits or even no sales.

In the past it is the advantage of being an experienced writer. You are aware of the significance in composing sentences that are coherent or proofreading. Editing, editing, and proofreading You are ready to start.

However, you'll still commit mistakes, but don't lose your vigilance. If you make mistakes most likely, they will happen during the sales procedure. What can you do to avoid costly errors?

DO make sure you have a captivating cover. If you've ever already sold ebooks then you've got an extra perk to have. It's the possibility to design a cover, or even the contact info of graphic designers.

Follow the same process that you used to design the previous covers for ebooks. If you're not experienced designing graphics, get an experienced professional. Your cover will be the first thing customers are exposed to in Amazon's Kindle Store. Amazon Kindle Store.

Don't assume that you've got a great cover. In the past, Kindle Store shoppers will be the first to see your book's cover. This is why it must be of high quality.

An unprofessionally designed or constructed cover is a big turn off. If the cover seems to have been sloppy, customers are likely to assume that your written content is not up to scratch. Also, you should solicit comments. Make three or four different covers and get the people whom you are familiar with for their input.

Make sure that your book has the correct format. There are not all ebooks suitable for an Amazon Kindle device. The documents should be the format of digital text.

Fortunately, Amazon handles the conversion for the benefit of. However, you will have to begin with an HTML, Word, text or PDF document. The experts recommend using choosing an HTML document. If you're using Microsoft Word, keep your Word document in its original format or save it in HTML.

DO NOT assume that your document were properly loaded. After uploading your book to the digital text platform you are able to override the preview feature. Avoid this. Instead, you should read the book. Examine the formatting. There is a tendency for formatting issues to occur. It is possible to find broken pages, errors in formatting and much numerous other errors. It is important to identify them prior to they can be fixed.

Don't forget to provide numerous details regarding your ebook. Prior to converting your ebook into digital format, you should be required to provide information about the book. It includes the title, the author's name, description about the book's genre, descriptions, and so on.

Utilize this section to make the most of this section to your advantage. Recheck your title. Do you think it is a good description for the book you are writing? If yes, then move into the book's details. Give as much detail as you can. This is a great opportunity to convince potential buyers that you're book is the most enjoyable book they've ever read.

Do not set your prices excessively extravagantly. Amazon lets you decide the cost of you Kindle book. It gives you an opportunity that is unique, however you also have the chance to slip up. Set a fair price.

If the book you're writing is less than 50 pages in length, don't think you'll get anything more than 10 dollars. Be aware of the expense for the Kindle. It's expensive. After spending a significant amount for it, the owners do not want to pay 20 dollars for a book they want to go through. They can visit a bookstore for much less.

Market your book. Once you've written a description of the book, upload and then convert the file, and then set the price, it'll be listed in the Amazon Kindle Store within 24 hours. A lot of first-time authors opt to sit back and watch the sales start to appear.

Yes, you are able to achieve this. You can also continue marketing the Amazon Kindle book online and make more money.

So, whether you wrote writing books, articles or other content printed for print or the internet there is a high opportunity to earn money via your Amazon Kindle

Store. The problem is that the capacity to create a great book doesn't automatically result in revenue. Make sure you have a great cover, make sure you have the proper formatting and then market the book in your own way.

Pricing Your Product When Selling Are you an author that would like to release an ebook through Amazon Kindle? The procedure is simple. After you've written and proofread your manuscript, you can visit Amazon.com. Amazon electronic text service. In your account, type the details of your product, add and convert your file into digital text, determine the price for selling, then release your ebook. Within 24 hours, your book is available for purchase in Amazon's Kindle Store. Amazon Kindle Store.

Publishing ebooks to The Amazon Kindle Store is a very simple method writers can earn cash. If you've had experience writing ebooks or articles then it's straightforward to compose your ebook. The option is to use a prior book that you've created and market it through Amazon.com. It's as it you keep the right to sell it.

Even though Amazon's Amazon Kindle Store is a very easy method to earn by your creativity but there is no guarantee. If a book is being offered for sale doesn't mean that it is going to be purchased. Naturally, it's crucial to pick a high-quality publication and an appealing design, but the cost can make a difference.

However, most new Kindle authors commit a costly error. The mistake they make is charging excessively for their book. What price do you need to charge your ebook?

The answer is dependent, since there are many aspects to take into consideration:

Print

Amazon permits you to publish and covert your printed book. If you self-published and wrote your book, you own complete rights over the book's title. It is possible to visit the digital text platform to easily transform your files. If you do not own an original copy of the document then scan each page of your book.

If you decide to do this take a look at the pricing you have in place or previously. Amazon requires that printed books are sold at fair value costs. If, for instance, you offer the printed version of your book at $14.99 it shouldn't cost $19.99 to sell the book on Amazon.com.

Length

eBooks are available in a variety of lengths. Many non-fiction or fiction books contain at minimum 200 pages. However How-to guides could contain as little than 50 pages. The length of the ebook will affect the price you charge. The less pages you have is, the lower price you can price it. A good cost for selling a guide on how to do your part to stop global warming, which is 50 pages in length is $5.99.

The Competitors

If you write a How-to book or write a novel to be published on your Amazon Kindle Store, scout the competitors. Look up your particular genre within their catalog or browse for titles that are similar to yours. What's the average cost of selling? It is not necessary to oversell make sure you choose a cost which is within the range of other sellers.

Your Targeted Market

In the majority of cases people are more likely to spend more money on novels. When writing a How-to guide be sure to think about your market and what they are able to spend.

A good example is a guide to save on grocery bills is targeted at those who want to cut costs and boost savings. The majority of people do not wish to spend a fortune on the book. In the end, they're looking to cut costs.

Your Royalties

Amazon.com provides every Kindle Book author a 35 percentage royalty on each book that is sold. It may seem to be much. However, because you're selling your work on an established website, and focusing on a particular audience, it is likely to achieve certain revenue. Make sure that your pricing is sufficient to allow you to earn profits.

Chapter 12: The Advertising Your Amazon Kindle Ebook

After that, you'll find a variety of self-publishing opportunities, which includes Amazon Kindle books. If you love writing the written word, this chance is not just entertaining but can also be a lucrative source of revenue.

While it's nice to learn that you can self-publish books using your Amazon Kindle, you may require more information. It is the Amazon Kindle is a portable electronic reader that can be carried around on a handheld device.

The device is fitted with Whispernet that allows all users to search or browse through the Amazon Kindle bookstore. The owners then buy the books they like then it downloads automatically onto their devices even while on the move.

Why should you create self-published book for Amazon's Amazon Kindle platform? Since you will earn a profit. Once you've written your product's details and uploading the files to digital conversion You decide on the price for sale. Because Amazon manages the sale and payment, they will pay the seller 35% of commissions for each sale as stated in its Terms and conditions. In contrast to other opportunities for making money it is not necessary to make an investment. You can list an ebook that is digital on Amazon. Amazon site.

Another reason to attempt to make money through selling and writing ebooks on Amazon Kindle ebook is that these devices are extremely highly regarded. Like we said, Kindle owners can access books from their mobile devices. It doesn't require cables. Also, as it is a portable device that Kindle weights less many book covers, it's an absolute huge success!

Amazon is having a hard time to keep the devices on stock. This is a sign of the amount of interest Amazon Kindle is and how the potential is huge for profit.

You may already be aware, Amazon is a popular marketplace on the internet. Retailers and users of the internet are able to buy and sell items on the site.

Because Amazon is already an established site, it works in your favor. The owners of the Kindle browse in the Amazon store for titles they love.

In essence, Amazon not only handles the selling of your book but also promotes the book through their website. Because it's a well-known site, it is likely to receive many page views and even the sales.

Although Amazon is a reputable site, it is still a good idea to promote your book. If you follow a few easy actions, you will generate more interest. This is the reason why you will see increased sales.

You can make cash by simply placing you Amazon Kindle book sell on Amazon's website however, why don't you take other steps to improve the profits you make?

Like we said, there are a variety of options available which are simple:

Online Boards of Message Boards

If you are a writer to earn money or to keep a job it is possible to join various online communities or message boards. Make use of this. The majority of websites have a buy sell or trade section. Write a message stating that you've written a novel to be published on the Amazon

Kindle and post a hyperlink to your sales page.

A lot of message boards permit signatures. They are links and messages appearing at the end of every blog post. The title of your book, and then make it clickable, leading to your sales webpage.

Article Directories

Article directories are sites which are both content-based and powered by users. Writers create articles and put links at the end of their article. If, for instance, you're selling a book about operating a daycare center, compose an article on doing the same. Offer tips for daycare providers.

Then, at the end of your piece, add something like "In simple terms, operating an enterprise daycare to make money is a straightforward and satisfying method to earn money working at your home." Write the word "running the daycare profitably," a clickable link which will lead directly to the Amazon selling page.

Sales Page

In terms of a sales webpage make your personal. You can use the descriptions you have provided Amazon using and then transfer the description to a brand new site or blog. Make sure you highlight the price of sale and add a link to your sales webpage.

Self-publishing an book for an Amazon Kindle platform is an simple and enjoyable option to earn money working at the comfort of your own home. With the popularity of Amazon it is possible to make some money. However, you must apply a few strategies for marketing by yourself to boost your earnings.

How to Market the "For Sale" Kindle Ebook

Did you write then covert and uploaded your ebook to your Amazon Kindle Store? If yes, you're currently selling a digital Kindle Book. The ebook will be on purchase through Amazon.com. While Amazon is an extremely popular site which receives lots of visitors, you must continue to market your book. Marketing can generate an interest. A good interest will translate to more sales.

How do you sell a sales Amazon Kindle ebook?

Create a Sales Page. In the past, Amazon Kindle Book is in electronic text format. In the event that you offer your book for sale Amazon will automatically cover your documents to protect the price you pay. It is recommended to keep the original file in your computer.

Utilize the original to create an original ebook. Make use of a free PDF converter online, or sign up using Create an account with PDF Online. Traditional eBooks must be offered in this format since the majority of computers have the necessary software to read.

After you convert your Microsoft Word file into an Adobe PDF file, you can create the selling page. This website can be created by yourself. The site can be as small as a single page. Write your own press release.

In the description, you should mention the title of your book, as well as your name as the creator as well as a brief the description. The description must include the plot, or areas covered in a guide.

Go to PayPal.com to sign up for a no-cost account. Offer your book for sale using PayPal (also Stripe) as an accepted payment method. This method allows you to make more money since you are targeting every computer owner in addition to those using Amazon Kindle. Amazon Kindle.

In the end of your sales page say that your ebook is to purchase for Amazon Kindle. Amazon Kindle device. Mention the selling price, and include a hyperlink on the Amazon selling page.

Make use of search engine optimization on your website's sales page. Search engine optimization includes using keyword-related articles. Internet users browse Yahoo or Google using these keywords.

Are the books a practical tutorial on slashing costs? Make use of a keyword tracker free instrument, which is located using a normal Internet search. Type in "save," or "save money." The tool will reveal precisely what keywords people search for. Integrate these on your website's sales page.

It allows search engines to find your website's contents. Therefore, when an online user is searching for "how to cut costs for groceries" they could be directed straight to your selling page.

They can buy the classic ebook, or go to Amazon.com to purchase Amazon.com for Kindle version.

Include testimonials from customers on your page of sales for ebooks. If you sell an Kindle Book on Amazon.com, customers will read your book.

However, it can be challenging to start. Many buyers aren't ready to buy an ebook without having read reviews before buying. If your book doesn't have reviews review, they might go elsewhere. Stop this from happening through obtaining customer reviews.

Make a post on Craigslist.org for users to look over your book. You can offer them a complimentary copy. Include their reviews on your sales page as well as in the description of the book on you Amazon Kindle Book.

Be active in the book or Amazon Kindle communities. There are numerous message boards on the internet that provide a variety of subjects. Searching on the internet will assist you in finding discussion boards on ebooks as well as other topics like the Amazon Kindle. Join these forums and become active.

Take part in discussion forums or start your own. If the forum includes an buy, sell or trade tab, you can list the details of your Amazon Kindle book for sale and add a link to the sale webpage. If you are allowed to sign your book you can create a catchy tagline to promote the Amazon Kindle book and make your link clickable. This will lead to your Amazon.com sale page.

As a result, it could be quite difficult to sell an available Amazon Kindle book. This is why you need to make a sales page that sells the traditional eBook as well. If you mention on your personal selling page that the book can also be purchased on the Amazon Kindle, you increase the amount you earn.

www.ingramcontent.com/pod-product-compliance
Lightning Source LLC
Chambersburg PA
CBHW071446080526
44587CB00014B/2015